THE ONTOLOGICAL ARGUMENT

ALVIN PLANTINGA is on leave from his position as associate professor of philosophy at Wayne State University in Detroit, to teach at Calvin College (Grand Rapids, Michigan), where he received his A.B. degree in 1954. He holds an M.A. from the University of Michigan and a Ph.D. from Yale University. He has also taught at the University of Illinois and at Harvard, and is the editor of a book, *Faith and Philosophy* (1964). A number of his articles have been published in philosophical journals.

RICHARD TAYLOR is a member of the Graduate Faculty at Columbia University. He holds an A.B. from the University of Illinois, an M.A. from Oberlin College, and a Ph.D. from Brown University, where he was named the first William Herbert Perry Faunce Professor of Philosophy. He has also taught at Swarthmore College and at Cornell and Ohio State universities. He is the author of *Metaphysics* (1963) and of many articles, and the editor of *The Will to Live: Selected Writings of Arthur Schopenhauer* (Anchor A266: 1962).

The Ontological Argument

FROM ST. ANSELM TO CONTEMPORARY
PHILOSOPHERS

Edited by
ALVIN PLANTINGA

With an Introduction by
RICHARD TAYLOR

Anchor Books
Doubleday & Company, Inc.
Garden City, New York

The Anchor Books edition is the first publication
of *The Ontological Argument*

Anchor Books edition: 1965

Library of Congress Catalog Card Number 65–10634

CONTENTS

INTRODUCTION

The ontological argument purports to prove, simply from the concept of God as the supreme being, that God's existence cannot rationally be doubted by anyone having such a concept of Him. It is thus a purely *a priori* argument, that is to say, one that does not appeal to any facts of experience but is concerned solely with the implications of concepts—in this case, the concept of God.

This argument has held a profound fascination for men since it was first so thoroughly and beautifully formulated by St. Anselm of Canterbury in the eleventh century. Few philosophical arguments have been the target of more attacks, and yet it finds new defenders among the ablest thinkers in every generation. Some critics have considered it hardly more than a play upon words and are apt to agree with Schopenhauer, who dismissed it as nothing but a "charming joke." Others, while rejecting the argument, have nevertheless treated it with the profoundest respect, considering it a credit to the wisdom and philosophical penetration of its inventor even though it does not, in their view, supply any rational basis for religious belief. Such was Immanuel Kant's opinion, for this philosopher thought he found in it the basis of all metaphysical arguments for God's existence, all of which he thought were inconclusive. At the other extreme are those philosophers, always in the minority but nonetheless sure of their insight, who consider it true not only that God, conceived as the supreme being, does indeed exist but that St. Anselm has rationally proved it.

It is doubtful whether this dispute will ever be settled to the satisfaction of all thinkers. Every reader must decide for himself the validity of this extraordinary proof and its importance. He will find among his predecessors a great diversity of views and interpretations. Certainly much more will be said about this argument in generations to come, although probably most tenable views are anticipated in the discussions presented in this collection.

The Origin of the Argument. St. Anselm did not use the expression "ontological argument." It was apparently first applied to his formulation by Kant, although Kant's predecessor, Christian Wolff, had popularized the term "ontologia." It is everywhere now used to refer, however, to an argument first developed in St. Anselm's *Proslogion.* In another work, the *Monologion,* St. Anselm constructed a variety of arguments for God's existence, basing them mainly upon certain features of creation. Some of these have won wider acceptance among philosophers and theologians than his more famous ontological argument, but they were not entirely original with St. Anselm and he is, accordingly, seldom referred to in connection with them. He was, however, undoubtedly the first author of the ontological argument and his name is rarely omitted from any discussion of it.

St. Anselm has recorded, in the *Proslogion,* how he came to construct his famous argument. He was, he writes, seeking some single argument that would not only prove God's existence but make evident God's attributes as well. The central idea of the ontological argument, that perfection implies existence, kept forcing itself upon him, but he rejected it as a specious and illusory basis for any argument until, finally, he realized he could find no rational ground for rejecting it any longer, whereupon he joyfully embraced it as providing the proof he had been seeking.

St. Anselm set forth his argument as an address to God. It is obvious, then, that he was not attempting to discover whether God exists. He was already perfectly convinced by faith of the reality of the Judaic-Christian God, conceived as a supreme being. His argument thus represents his attempt to understand, by his mind or reason, that which he already firmly believed by his faith or, as he expressed it, in his heart. On the other hand, he makes it perfectly clear that it is intended to be a philosophical proof and not merely an expression of pious persuasion. His argument presupposes no belief in the existence of God. It presupposes only the concept of God, that is to say, the concept of an absolutely supreme being, and for this no religious faith at all is required.

St. Anselm's Arguments. Actually, St. Anselm formulated what appear to be two arguments, the conclusions of which are not exactly the same. It is unfortunate that so few have realized that two distinct arguments can be made out in his writing, and that the rejection of one of these might leave the other still quite untouched. Indeed, it was apparently not clear even to St. Anselm himself that he was mixing together two quite different arguments. The first of these purports to show that it follows, just from the concept of God, that God does exist. The second makes the stronger claim that God exists necessarily, or in other words, that God possesses a kind of existence that is possessed by no other thing. It was essentially the first argument that was subsequently developed with such clarity by Descartes, and largely for this reason it is this version that has received the most celebrated and devastating criticism.

The First Argument. St. Anselm's first argument is, roughly, to this effect. We think of God as the supreme being; or at least, all men should so think of Him. Ignorant men may, to be sure, call the sun and the moon and other things in creation "God," but it is part of the Judaic-Christian tradition that God is the supreme being. In any case God can be so conceived even by those who do not believe in Him, provided, of course, that they are not fools. Now by the supreme being is meant not merely whatever, among all the things there are, happens to be greatest or best, for that could indeed turn out to be the sun or the moon or some other part of creation, in case no God exists. By "the supreme being" is meant, on the contrary, the greatest *possible* being, in case there is any such. In St. Anselm's celebrated phrase, God must be thought of as "a being than which nothing greater can be *conceived.*" To St. Anselm, as to Descartes much later, it appeared that a being so described could not fail to exist. If such a being happened not to exist, then it would not be the greatest one could conceive, for one can conceive of such a being as possessing existence, and the existent is plainly greater than the non-existent. Indeed, a God devoid of existence would have even less worth or significance than any real thing, however trifling. A crude and inadequate but perhaps graphic way of expressing this idea would be to say that no non-existent thing is in the least worthy of worship and could not possibly be considered the supreme being. God, whatever else He may be, must be a reality as the very minimum condition of being thought of as God.

It is in somewhat this fashion that the ontological argument is usually represented, and it is often assumed that St. Anselm was saying little more than this. No doubt it is contained in what he said, though later, in replying to the criticisms of his contemporary Gaunilo, he appeared to deny that it was even a part of his argument. There can be little question, however, that this expresses the central idea in Descartes' subsequent formulation of the argument, so before returning to St. Anselm we should perhaps turn briefly to Descartes.

Descartes' Formulation. St. Anselm, we noted, began with a firm belief in God, derived from his faith, and even expressed his argument in more or less the form of a prayer. He thought that anyone who, like himself, had a clear idea of God could not possibly doubt His existence. If anyone doubts God's existence he shows only that he is a fool, like the fool mentioned in the Psalm (14) who says in his heart that there is no God. His foolishness consists, however, not in his being a bad philosopher, but in his having an inadequate conception of God.

Descartes' emphasis was somewhat different. His purpose was purely philosophical, and instead of addressing his thoughts to God, he addressed them to the doubter, personified in himself. His reflections are not those of a believer seeking understanding, but rather of a philosopher seeking truth, in order that belief might follow. Descartes needed a demonstration of God's existence, and with it God's trustworthiness or veracity, to banish his own philosophical skepticism and establish the reality of a material world that he had professed to find himself capable of doubting.

Descartes thought that the only sure way to metaphysical truth and certainty was through the formation of clear and distinct ideas and the rational analysis of them, a procedure that he believed emulated the method of geometry and held promise of yielding the same certitude. Conceiving of God as a "supremely perfect being," he noted that he possessed a clear idea of such a being, within himself. To discover the nature of God, then, he had only to discover what was contained in this idea. He found that the idea of existence was inseparable from the idea of God, that his conception of God was the conception of a being whose existence was inseparable, even in thought, from God's very nature or essence. Another way in which he expressed this was by asserting that God, being supremely perfect, cannot be thought of except as embodying every perfection. For Descartes, however, existence is itself a perfection, and so it follows that God cannot even be thought of except as a real being. Existence is not, however, contained in the idea of anything else; whatever I might form an idea of, Descartes thought, I can always conceive to be non-existent at some time or other, with the sole exception of God. No absurdity is involved in saying of a winged horse, for instance, either that it does or that it does not exist, nor in saying even of oneself that at some time or other that self does not exist. Considering God, however, Descartes maintained that one can no more conceive Him as non-existent than one can conceive a plane triangle whose angles are not equal to the sum of two right angles. If one affirms that what he is thinking of does not have angles equal to the sum of two right angles then it follows either that his idea of a triangle is unclear, or that he is thinking, perhaps clearly, of something other than a triangle. Similarly, if one affirms that God does not exist then it follows either that he is not applying the name "God" to a supremely perfect being, or that his idea of God is very unclear.

The Traditional Criticism of This Argument. Few philosophers have considered this a very good argument. The best-known exceptions are Leibniz and Spinoza, both of whom, however, introduced considerable modifications of their own. Schopenhauer considered the argument nothing more than a bit of philosophical prestidigitation, comparable to a magician's producing a rabbit from a hat. The magician, of course, first puts the rabbit into the hat, while the attention of the audience is diverted, and the defender of the ontological argument, Schopenhauer thought, similarly slips "God exists" into his premises somewhere, concealing this as best he can ("for decency's sake") in order to have the specious triumph of producing it in his conclusion. This kind of criticism was anticipated hundreds of years earlier, however, by Gaunilo, the monk who commented on St. Anselm's writing. Gaunilo noted that it is quite possible to have in one's mind all manner of unreal, chimerical beings, like beautiful islands that no one has ever beheld because they nowhere exist. One cannot raise them into existence merely by conceiving of them as surpassingly beautiful, or even as perfect; nor is this accomplished by inconspicuously slipping the idea of existence into one's original notion of perfection.

Kant's Criticism. In any case it is fairly easy to see why such an argument is so singularly unconvincing, and why Schopenhauer contemptuously dismissed it as hardly more than a joke. Kant expressed the refutation best in his claim that existence is no *predicate.* There is, to be sure, a great difference between things that exist and those that do not, but Kant insisted that our ideas or conceptions of them are exactly the same in either case. Having described a thing, no matter what, one adds nothing to the description of it, according to Kant, by adding that it exists. There is no contradiction in denying of anything whatever, including a being than which no greater can be conceived, that it exists. A contradiction arises, Kant insisted, only when incompatible properties are predicated of one and the same thing. The denial that God exists, however, involves no such predication. On the contrary, it amounts to a refusal to ascribe those properties conceived of as possessed by God to anything whatever, and no contradiction can result from that.

Such is the substance of Kant's criticism, and virtually all thinkers since have considered it apt, at least as applied to Descartes' version of the argument. No one, it is now generally thought, can pass from the mere conception or idea of a thing to the conclusion that the thing thus conceived actually exists or that it does not exist. Some proof of existence is needed that a mere description, however exalted, does not supply.

St. Anselm's Second Argument. It has already been noted that there are important differences between the arguments of St. Anselm and Descartes, and that these differences are too seldom noted. Norman Malcolm has pointed out that a line of thought significantly different from the foregoing is found in St. Anselm's *Proslogion* and in his reply to Gaunilo. Following Malcolm, we shall refer to this as St. Anselm's second argument.

Two Kinds of Existence. To appreciate this second argument it is important to understand first a distinction between two senses of existence. The first kind of existence was referred to by St. Anselm and other scholastics as existence *in intellectu.* To say of anything that it exists *in intellectu*—roughly, in the understanding—is to say nothing more than that a clear idea of it exists, or that someone rightly understands a description that he is given. Thus do winged horses, griffins, unicorns and so on exist, *in intellectu,* together with horses, the sun and the moon and so on, for all these things, whether they actually exist or not, can be clearly described and the descriptions of them conveyed to one's understanding. Such things, moreover, as square circles, colorless bodies and fire that is without heat can exist *in intellectu,* for these too can be described and accurately defined and the definitions and descriptions of them understood. Indeed, unless one understood what is meant by, say, a square circle—namely, an equal four-sided plane figure all of whose points are equidistant from its center—he could not know with certainty that nothing answering to that description exists anywhere in reality, for he simply would not, under those conditions, understand what it was whose real existence was being denied. This brings out the additional point that to have an idea of something, or better, to have a clear concept of it, is not the same as having some sort of mental picture or image of it. No one can form an image of a square circle. Or, to use Descartes' example, no one can really form an image of a plane figure having exactly one thousand equal sides. Yet we can certainly understand what these things are and often with such perfect clarity that we can deduce with absolute certainty some properties not mentioned in the definitions of them. From the clear concept of a rectilinear triangle, for example, one can deduce that the sum of its smaller angles is equal to its greater angle. From the clear concept of a square circle one can immediately and with absolute certainty deduce that no such thing can exist in reality.

The second kind of existence was referred to by St. Anselm and other scholastics as existence *in re*. This is what is ordinarily meant by existence; namely, real, as opposed to imaginary, existence. It is in this sense that the sun and moon and earth exist, while the golden mountain, the Islands of the Blest and the satellites of Mercury do not.

It should be clear that these two modes of existence are not mutually exclusive. Something might exist in either sense but not the other, or in both senses, or in neither. The sun, for example, exists *in re*, but also *in intellectu*, for we understand what is meant by the sun. The satellites of Mercury, on the other hand, exist *in intellectu* but not *in re*, since Mercury has no satellites. There are, moreover, surely things that exist *in re* but not *in intellectu*; namely, all those real beings as yet undiscovered by men, of which they have formed no conception. Anything, finally, which is unreal and of which no man has ever framed a conception has no existence of either kind. If a man were for the first time to fabricate a description of some unreal and hitherto undreamed of thing, something of which no man had ever before formed a conception, then that thing would thereupon exist in that man's understanding, but until then it would have had no existence at all, even *in intellectu*.

Now clearly, God exists *in intellectu*; that is, God exists in the understanding of men, provided that they are not fools. Anyone except a fool can grasp the idea of a supreme being, that is to say, a being of such greatness that no greater being could possibly be, or even be conceived. At least so it seemed to St. Anselm, for this is the very conception of God that believers are supposed to possess. Nothing less could properly be deemed a *supreme* being in the sense understood in the Judaic-Christian tradition.

The Transition from Idea to Thing. Can one, however, fairly pass from the conception of such a being, or its existence *in intellectu*, to either the affirmation or the denial of its real existence? The possibility of doing so is often dismissed out of hand, which amounts to dismissing the basic feature of the ontological argument.

Yet as a matter of fact all men are perfectly accustomed to making this transition when it comes to *denying* the existence *in re* of certain things. Thus, from one's clear understanding of what is meant by a plane four-sided figure, all of whose points are equidistant from the center, one can conclude with certainty that no such being exists in reality. The propriety of doing so is never questioned by anyone, and yet it is a clear instance of drawing a conclusion concerning what does or does not exist in reality solely from the clear conception of something in one's understanding. Nor is this a case of "defining something out of existence," which would be the reverse of what St. Anselm is often accused of doing. It is simply a case of showing, solely from the description of a thing, that the thing in question is impossible, and properly concluding from this that it does not, therefore, exist. Critics of the ontological argument who have deemed it obvious that one can never legitimately pass from the mere description of something to any conclusion concerning the existence in reality of the thing described have simply failed to note that this is not only a legitimate inference but a very common one when it is the non-existence of something that is inferred. One might maintain that God's existence cannot be proved by a consideration of the concept of God, but one cannot do so on the ground that *no* conclusions concerning what exists can be derived solely from our conceptions of things, for that is not true.

Contingent, Necessary, and Impossible Existence. It should be noted next that when one establishes the non-existence of something, such as a square circle, simply from his understanding of what such a thing would be in case it did exist, he establishes something much stronger than the claim that such a thing does not, in fact, exist in this or that place or time. He establishes that it cannot exist, or that its non-existence is necessary, and hence that it necessarily exists nowhere and at no time.

This introduces further distinctions that are basic to understanding St. Anselm's thought; namely, the distinctions between *contingent* existence or non-existence, *impossible* existence, and *necessary* existence. A thing exists contingently if it exists, but is such that there is no logical absurdity in affirming that it does not. The British Isles exist contingently. They are real, but there is no difficulty in conceiving of a world without them. A thing is contingently non-existent in case it does not exist, but is such that there is no logical absurdity in affirming that it does. The non-existence of Mercury's satellite, for instance, is contingent. The satellite is not real, but there is no difficulty in conceiving that it is. The non-existence of a square circle, on the other hand, is necessary; that is, its existence is impossible. It would be an understatement to say merely that no such thing exists anywhere, for it is, in scholastic terminology, of its very essence or nature not to exist. Any being so described is at once seen to be an impossible being.

St. Anselm's arguments and the torrent of philosophy they have generated should be understood in the light of these basic ideas. The idea of necessary non-existence or, better, impossible existence, presents little difficulty. We can apply this notion to anything, such as a square circle, which is non-existent by its very nature. It exists *in intellectu*, for anyone can understand a clear definition of such a thing though he cannot, of course, comprehend it.

But from one's very understanding of it he can be certain that no such thing exists *in re*. It is eternally and ubiquitously non-existent, or cannot exist anywhere or at any time. For the proof of this one need not seek such beings and fail to find them anywhere. One need not go beyond the conception of such a being. It is not thereby defined out of existence, for it can have no existence to lose. Nor does one need, in proving the non-existence of such a being, surreptitiously to slip into one's proof the *premise* that it does not exist. Its non-existence is perfectly evident to anyone who understands what is being described, and no one but a fool could be a believer in such a being.

God as a Necessary Being. It seemed to St. Anselm that the idea of impossible non-existence, or better, necessary existence, is also perfectly comprehensible. It is but the corollary of the foregoing, though he did not put it in these terms. We can apply this notion to anything that exists by its very nature, in case the clear conception of such a thing can be formed. One can form a clear conception of God, conceived as the supreme being, or a being of such greatness that none greater can either be or be conceived. St. Anselm had no doubt that such a being exists *in intellectu,* for anyone but a fool can understand a clear description of God, though of course no one can comprehend such a being any more than he can comprehend the idea of a square circle. And from one's understanding of it one can, it was clear to St. Anselm, be certain that such a being exists *in re.* It is eternally and ubiquitously existent, and cannot fail to exist anywhere or at any time. For the proof of this, St. Anselm maintained, one need not find such a being; one need not go beyond the conception of it. God is not thereby defined into existence, any more than square circles are defined out of existence, for He can no more *gain* existence than a square circle can lose it. Nor does one need, in proving the existence of such a being, surreptitiously to slip into one's proof the premise that it exists. Its existence is perfectly evident to anyone who really understands what is being described, and only a fool, St. Anselm said, or one who has no clear understanding of what is meant by God can fail to believe in Him.

Such are the basic suppositions of the ontological argument. It has fascinated thinkers, particularly those of a rationalistic sentiment, for centuries, and has equally won the scorn of those who try to derive all human knowledge from sense experience. Perhaps in matters of theology more than in most others the feelings and sentiments of men are the fathers of their ideas and beliefs, determining for them in advance what conclusions they will accept or reject, but St. Anselm's argument, which has here been only barely adumbrated, makes no appeal to the feelings. It rests its conclusion solely on its claim of validity. Whether or not it ever convinces a theological doubter, it will always remain one of the boldest creations of man's reason and a credit not only to its inventor, but to human reason itself.

Richard Taylor

New York City
March 25, 1964

PART I

THE ONTOLOGICAL ARGUMENT IN THE HISTORY OF PHILOSOPHY

1. ST. ANSELM (1033–1109)

[*St. Anselm, the Archbishop of Canterbury, is rightly regarded as the inventor and perfecter of the ontological argument, though his philosophical inspiration was largely derived from St. Augustine. His position is not that of a skeptic seeking some rational persuasion of God's existence, but that of a believer seeking a single conception which would make manifest at once God's existence and God's attributes. He accordingly prefaced the arguments that follow with the famous pronouncement: "I do not endeavor, O Lord, to penetrate thy sublimity, for in no wise do I compare my understanding with that; but I long to understand in some degree thy truth, which my heart believes and loves. For I do not seek to understand that I may believe, but I believe in order to understand. For this also I believe,—that unless I believed, I should not understand."*]

A. ST. ANSELM'S ONTOLOGICAL ARGUMENT*

CHAPTER II.

Truly there is a God, although the fool hath said in his heart, There is no God.

And so, Lord, do thou, who dost give understanding to faith, give me, so far as thou knowest it to be profitable, to

* Chapters II–IV of St. Anselm's *Proslogion*. This and the two selections that follow are from *Anselm's Basic Writings*, translated by S. N. Deane, with an introduction by Charles Hartshorne, 2nd edition, 1962, and are reprinted by permission of The Open Court Publishing Company.

understand that thou art as we believe; and that thou art that which we believe. And, indeed, we believe that thou art a being than which nothing greater can be conceived. Or is there no such nature, since the fool hath said in his heart, there is no God? (Psalm xiv. 1). But, at any rate, this very fool, when he hears of this being of which I speak —a being than which nothing greater can be conceived— understands what he hears, and what he understands is in his understanding; although he does not understand it to exist.

For, it is one thing for an object to be in the understanding, and another to understand that the object exists. When a painter first conceives of what he will afterwards perform, he has it in his understanding, but he does not yet understand it to be, because he has not yet performed it. But after he has made the painting, he both has it in his understanding, and he understands that it exists, because he has made it.

Hence, even the fool is convinced that something exists in the understanding, at least, than which nothing greater can be conceived. For, when he hears of this, he understands it. And whatever is understood, exists in the understanding. And assuredly that, than which nothing greater can be conceived, cannot exist in the understanding alone. For, suppose it exists in the understanding alone: then it can be conceived to exist in reality; which is greater.

Therefore, if that, than which nothing greater can be conceived, exists in the understanding alone, the very being, than which nothing greater can be conceived, is one, than which a greater can be conceived. But obviously this is impossible. Hence, there is no doubt that there exists a being, than which nothing greater can be conceived, and it exists both in the understanding and in reality.

CHAPTER III.

God cannot be conceived not to exist.—God is that, than which nothing greater can be conceived.—That which can be conceived not to exist is not God.

And it assuredly exists so truly, that it cannot be conceived not to exist. For, it is possible to conceive of a being which cannot be conceived not to exist; and this is greater than one which can be conceived not to exist. Hence, if that, than which nothing greater can be conceived, can be conceived not to exist, it is not that, than which nothing greater can be conceived. But this is an irreconcilable contradiction. There is, then, so truly a being than which nothing greater can be conceived to exist, that it cannot even be conceived not to exist; and this being thou art, O Lord, our God.

So truly, therefore, dost thou exist, O Lord, my God, that thou canst not be conceived not to exist; and rightly. For, if a mind could conceive of a being better than thee, the creature would rise above the Creator; and this is most absurd. And, indeed, whatever else there is, except thee alone, can be conceived not to exist. To thee alone, therefore, it belongs to exist more truly than all other beings, and hence in a higher degree than all others. For, whatever else exists does not exist so truly, and hence in a less degree it belongs to it to exist. Why, then, has the fool said in his heart, there is no God (Psalm xiv. 1), since it is so evident, to a rational mind, that thou dost exist in the highest degree of all? Why, except that he is dull and a fool?

CHAPTER IV.

How the fool has said in his heart what cannot be conceived.—A thing may be conceived in two ways: (1) when the word signifying it is conceived; (2) when the thing itself is understood. As far as the word goes, God can be conceived not to exist; in reality he cannot.

But how has the fool said in his heart what he could not conceive; or how is it that he could not conceive what he said in his heart? since it is the same to say in the heart, and to conceive.

But, if really, nay, since really, he both conceived, because he said in his heart; and did not say in his heart, because he could not conceive; there is more than one way in which a thing is said in the heart or conceived. For, in one sense, an object is conceived, when the word signifying it is conceived; and in another, when the very entity, which the object is, is understood.

In the former sense, then, God can be conceived not to exist; but in the latter, not at all. For no one who understands what fire and water are can conceive fire to be water, in accordance with the nature of the facts themselves, although this is possible according to the words. So, then, no one who understands what God is can conceive that God does not exist, although he says these words in his heart, either without any, or with some foreign, signification. For, God is that than which a greater cannot be conceived. And he who thoroughly understands this, assuredly understands that this being so truly exists, that not even in concept can it be non-existent. Therefore, he who understands that God so exists, cannot conceive that he does not exist.

I thank thee, gracious Lord, I thank thee; because what I formerly believed by thy bounty, I now so understand by thine illumination, that if I were unwilling to believe that thou dost exist, I should not be able not to understand this to be true.

B. GAUNILO (DATES UNKNOWN): *IN BEHALF OF THE FOOL*

[Gaunilo, a contemporary of St. Anselm, was a monk of Marmoutier and accordingly a believer, like St. Anselm. Apart from his famous reply to St. Anselm, little, if anything, is now known of him. He did not reject St. Anselm's conclusion that God exists, for of this he was already entirely convinced, but he protested against what seemed to him a specious argument for that conclusion. It appeared to Gaunilo, as it has to many since, that St. Anselm was merely defining God into existence, that by similar reasoning one could "prove" the existence of anything he pleased. St. Anselm had maintained that only a fool, or

*someone who could form no clear conception of God,
could really doubt His existence. Gaunilo, accordingly, entitled his reply to St. Anselm* In Behalf of the Fool, *and
endeavored to show how such a man, though foolish,
might nevertheless be right.*]

1. If one doubts or denies the existence of a being of
such a nature that nothing greater than it can be conceived, he receives this answer:

The existence of this being is proved, in the first place,
by the fact that he himself, in his doubt or denial regarding
this being, already has it in his understanding; for in hearing it spoken of he understands what is spoken of. It is
proved, therefore, by the fact that what he understands
must exist not only in his understanding, but in reality also.

And the proof of this is as follows.—It is a greater thing
to exist both in the understanding and in reality than to
be in the understanding alone. And if this being is in the
understanding alone, whatever has even in the past existed
in reality will be greater than this being. And so that
which was greater than all beings will be less than some
being, and will not be greater than all: which is a manifest
contradiction.

And hence, that which is greater than all, already
proved to be in the understanding, must exist not only in
the understanding, but also in reality: for otherwise it will
not be greater than all other beings.

2. The fool might make this reply:

This being is said to be in my understanding already,
only because I understand what is said. Now could it not
with equal justice be said that I have in my understanding
all manner of unreal objects, having absolutely no existence
in themselves, because I understand these things if one
speaks of them, whatever they may be?

Unless indeed it is shown that this being is of such a
character that it cannot be held in concept like all unreal
objects, or objects whose existence is uncertain: and hence
I am not able to conceive of it when I hear of it, or to
hold it in concept; but I must understand it and have it in
my understanding; because, it seems, I cannot conceive

of it in any other way than by understanding it, that is, by comprehending in my knowledge its existence in reality.

But if this is the case, in the first place there will be no distinction between what has precedence in time—namely, the having of an object in the understanding—and what is subsequent in time—namely, the understanding that an object exists; as in the example of the picture, which exists first in the mind of the painter, and afterwards in his work.

Moreover, the following assertion can hardly be accepted: that this being, when it is spoken of and heard of, cannot be conceived not to exist in the way in which even God can be conceived not to exist. For if this is impossible, what was the object of this argument against one who doubts or denies the existence of such a being?

Finally, that this being so exists that it cannot be perceived by an understanding convinced of its own indubitable existence, unless this being is afterwards conceived of—this should be proved to me by an indisputable argument, but not by that which you have advanced: namely, that what I understand, when I hear it, already is in my understanding. For thus in my understanding, as I still think, could be all sorts of things whose existence is uncertain, or which do not exist at all, if some one whose words I should understand mentioned them. And so much the more if I should be deceived, as often happens, and believe in them: though I do not yet believe in the being whose existence you would prove.

3. Hence, your example of the painter who already has in his understanding what he is to paint cannot agree with this argument. For the picture, before it is made, is contained in the artificer's art itself; and any such thing, existing in the art of an artificer, is nothing but a part of his understanding itself. A joiner, St. Augustine says, when he is about to make a box in fact, first has it in his art. The box which is made in fact is not life; but the box which exists in his art is life. For the artificer's soul lives, in which all these things are, before they are produced. Why, then, are these things life in the living soul of the artificer, unless because they are nothing else than the knowledge or understanding of the soul itself?

With the exception, however, of those facts which are known to pertain to the mental nature, whatever, on being heard and thought out by the understanding, is perceived to be real, undoubtedly that real object is one thing, and the understanding itself, by which the object is grasped, is another. Hence, even if it were true that there is a being than which a greater is inconceivable: yet to this being, when heard of and understood, the not yet created picture in the mind of the painter is not analogous.

4. Let us notice also the point touched on above, with regard to this being which is greater than all which can be conceived, and which, it is said, can be none other than God himself. I, so far as actual knowledge of the object, either from its specific or general character, is concerned, am as little able to conceive of this being when I hear of it, or to have it in my understanding, as I am to conceive of or understand God himself: whom, indeed, for this very reason I can conceive not to exist. For I do not know that reality itself which God is, nor can I form a conjecture of that reality from some other like reality. For you yourself assert that that reality is such that there can be nothing else like it.

For, suppose that I should hear something said of a man absolutely unknown to me, of whose very existence I was unaware. Through that special or general knowledge by which I know what man is, or what men are, I could conceive of him also, according to the reality itself, which man is. And yet it would be possible, if the person who told me of him deceived me, that the man himself, of whom I conceived, did not exist; since that reality according to which I conceived of him, though a no less indisputable fact, was not that man, but any man.

Hence, I am not able, in the way in which I should have this unreal being in concept or in understanding, to have that being of which you speak in concept or in understanding, when I hear the word *God* or the words, *a being greater than all other beings.* For I can conceive of the man according to a fact that is real and familiar to me: but of God, or a being greater than all others, I could not conceive at all, except merely according to the word. And an object can hardly or never be conceived according to the word alone.

For when it is so conceived, it is not so much the word itself (which is, indeed, a real thing—that is, the sound of the letters and syllables) as the signification of the word, when heard, that is conceived. But it is not conceived as by one who knows what is generally signified by the word; by whom, that is, it is conceived according to a reality and in true conception alone. It is conceived as by a man who does not know the object, and conceives of it only in accordance with the movement of his mind produced by hearing the word, the mind attempting to image for itself the signification of the word that is heard. And it would be surprising if in the reality of fact it could ever attain to this.

Thus, it appears, and in no other way, this being is also in my understanding, when I hear and understand a person who says that there is a being greater than all conceivable beings. So much for the assertion that this supreme nature already is in my understanding.

5. But that this being must exist, not only in the understanding but also in reality, is thus proved to me:

If it did not so exist, whatever exists in reality would be greater than it. And so the being which has been already proved to exist in my understanding, will not be greater than all other beings.

I still answer: if it should be said that a being which cannot be even conceived in terms of any fact, is in the understanding, I do not deny that this being is, accordingly, in my understanding. But since through this fact it can in no wise attain to real existence also, I do not yet concede to it that existence at all, until some certain proof of it shall be given.

For he who says that this being exists, because otherwise the being which is greater than all will not be greater than all, does not attend strictly enough to what he is saying. For I do not yet say, no, I even deny or doubt that this being is greater than any real object. Nor do I concede to it any other existence than this (if it should be called existence) which it has when the mind, according to a word merely heard, tries to form the image of an object absolutely unknown to it.

How, then, is the veritable existence of that being proved to me from the assumption, by hypothesis, that it is greater than all other beings? For I should still deny this, or doubt your demonstration of it, to this extent, that I should not admit that this being is in my understanding and concept even in the way in which many objects whose real existence is uncertain and doubtful, are in my understanding and concept. For it should be proved first that this being itself really exists somewhere; and then, from the fact that it is greater than all, we shall not hesitate to infer that it also subsists in itself.

6. For example: it is said that somewhere in the ocean is an island, which, because of the difficulty, or rather the impossibility, of discovering what does not exist, is called the lost island. And they say that this island has an inestimable wealth of all manner of riches and delicacies in greater abundance than is told of the Islands of the Blest; and that having no owner or inhabitant, it is more excellent than all other countries, which are inhabited by mankind, in the abundance with which it is stored.

Now if some one should tell me that there is such an island, I should easily understand his words, in which there is no difficulty. But suppose that he went on to say, as if by a logical inference: "You can no longer doubt that this island which is more excellent than all lands exists somewhere, since you have no doubt that it is in your understanding. And since it is more excellent not to be in the understanding alone, but to exist both in the understanding and in reality, for this reason it must exist. For if it does not exist, any land which really exists will be more excellent than it; and so the island already understood by you to be more excellent will not be more excellent."

If a man should try to prove to me by such reasoning that this island truly exists, and that its existence should no longer be doubted, either I should believe that he was jesting, or I know not which I ought to regard as the greater fool: myself, supposing that I should allow this proof; or him, if he should suppose that he had established with any certainty the existence of this island. For he ought to show first that the hypothetical excellence of this island exists as a real and indubitable fact, and in no wise as any unreal object, or one whose existence is uncertain, in my understanding.

7. This, in the mean time, is the answer the fool could make to the arguments urged against him. When he is assured in the first place that this being is so great that its non-existence is not even conceivable, and that this in turn is proved on no other ground than the fact that otherwise it will not be greater than all things, the fool may make the same answer, and say:

When did I say that any such being exists in reality, that is, a being greater than all others?—that on this ground it should be proved to me that it also exists in reality to such a degree that it cannot even be conceived not to exist? Whereas in the first place it should be in some way proved that a nature which is higher, that is, greater and better, than all other natures, exists; in order that from this we may then be able to prove all attributes which necessarily the being that is greater and better than all possesses.

Moreover, it is said that the non-existence of this being is inconceivable. It might better be said, perhaps, that its non-existence, or the possibility of its non-existence, is unintelligible. For according to the true meaning of the word, unreal objects are unintelligible. Yet their existence is conceivable in the way in which the fool conceived of the non-existence of God. I am most certainly aware of my own existence; but I know, nevertheless, that my non-existence is possible. As to that supreme being, moreover, which God is, I understand without any doubt both his existence, and the impossibility of his non-existence. Whether, however, so long as I am most positively aware of my existence, I can conceive of my non-existence, I am not sure. But if I can, why can I not conceive of the non-existence of whatever else I know with the same certainty? If, however, I cannot, God will not be the only being of which it can be said, it is impossible to conceive of his non-existence.

8. The other parts of this book are argued with such truth, such brilliancy, such grandeur; and are so replete

with usefulness, so fragrant with a certain perfume of de-
vout and holy feeling, that though there are matters in
the beginning which, however rightly sensed, are weakly
presented, the rest of the work should not be rejected
on this account. The rather ought these earlier matters to
be reasoned more cogently, and the whole to be received
with great respect and honor.

C. ST. ANSELM'S REPLY TO GAUNILO

It was a fool against whom the argument of my Proslogium was directed. Seeing, however, that the author of
these objections is by no means a fool, and is a Catholic,
speaking in behalf of the fool, I think it sufficient that I
answer the Catholic.

CHAPTER I

A general refutation of Gaunilo's argument. It is
shown that a being than which a greater cannot be
conceived exists in reality.

You say—whosoever you may be, who say that a fool is
capable of making these statements—that a being than
which a greater cannot be conceived is not in the understanding in any other sense than that in which a being that
is altogether inconceivable in terms of reality, is in the
understanding. You say that the inference that this being
exists in reality, from the fact that it is in the understanding, is no more just than the inference that a lost island
most certainly exists, from the fact that when it is described the hearer does not doubt that it is in his understanding.

But I say: if a being than which a greater is inconceivable is not understood or conceived, and is not in the
understanding or in concept, certainly either God is not a
being than which a greater is inconceivable, or else he is
not understood or conceived, and is not in the understanding or in concept. But I call on your faith and conscience

to attest that this is most false. Hence, that than which a greater cannot be conceived is truly understood and conceived, and is in the understanding and in concept. Therefore either the grounds on which you try to controvert me are not true, or else the inference which you think to base logically on those grounds is not justified.

But you hold, moreover, that supposing that a being than which a greater cannot be conceived is understood, it does not follow that this being is in the understanding; nor, if it is in the understanding, does it therefore exist in reality.

In answer to this, I maintain positively: if that being can be even conceived to be, it must exist in reality. For that than which a greater is inconceivable cannot be conceived except as without beginning. But whatever can be conceived to exist, and does not exist, can be conceived to exist through a beginning. Hence what can be conceived to exist, but does not exist, is not the being than which a greater cannot be conceived. Therefore, if such a being can be conceived to exist, necessarily it does exist.

Furthermore: if it can be conceived at all, it must exist. For no one who denies or doubts the existence of a being than which a greater is inconceivable, denies or doubts that if it did exist, its non-existence, either in reality or in the understanding, would be impossible. For otherwise it would not be a being than which a greater cannot be conceived. But as to whatever can be conceived, but does not exist—if there were such a being, its non-existence, either in reality or in the understanding, would be possible. Therefore if a being than which a greater is inconceivable can be even conceived, it cannot be non-existent.

But let us suppose that it does not exist, even if it can be conceived. Whatever can be conceived, but does not exist, if it existed, would not be a being than which a greater is inconceivable. If, then, there were a being a greater than which is inconceivable, it would not be a being than which a greater is inconceivable: which is most absurd. Hence, it is false to deny that a being than which a greater cannot be conceived exists, if it can be even conceived; much the more, therefore, if it can be understood or can be in the understanding.

Moreover, I will venture to make this assertion: without doubt, whatever at any place or at any time does not exist—even if it does exist at some place or at some time—can be conceived to exist nowhere and never, as at some place and at some time it does not exist. For what did not exist yesterday, and exists to-day, as it is understood not to have existed yesterday, so it can be apprehended by the intelligence that it never exists. And what is not here, and is elsewhere, can be conceived to be nowhere, just as it is not here. So with regard to an object of which the individual parts do not exist at the same places or times: all its parts and therefore its very whole can be conceived to exist nowhere or never.

For, although time is said to exist always, and the world everywhere, yet time does not as a whole exist always, nor the world as a whole everywhere. And as individual parts of time do not exist when others exist, so they can be conceived never to exist. And so it can be apprehended by the intelligence that individual parts of the world exist nowhere, as they do not exist where other parts exist. Moreover, what is composed of parts can be dissolved in concept, and be non-existent. Therefore, whatever at any place or at any time does not exist as a whole, even if it is existent, can be conceived not to exist.

But that than which a greater cannot be conceived, if it exists, cannot be conceived not to exist. Otherwise, it is not a being than which a greater cannot be conceived: which is inconsistent. By no means, then, does it at any place or at any time fail to exist as a whole: but it exists as a whole everywhere and always.

Do you believe that this being can in some way be conceived or understood, or that the being with regard to which these things are understood can be in concept or in the understanding? For if it cannot, these things cannot be understood with reference to it. But if you say that it is not understood and that it is not in the understanding, because it is not thoroughly understood; you should say that a man who cannot face the direct rays of the sun does not see the light of day, which is none other than the sunlight. Assuredly a being than which a greater cannot be conceived exists, and is in the understanding, at least to this extent—that these statements regarding it are understood.

CHAPTER II.

The argument is continued. It is shown that a being than which a greater is inconceivable can be conceived, and also, in so far, exists.

I have said, then, in the argument which you dispute, that when the fool hears mentioned a being than which a greater is inconceivable, he understands what he hears. Certainly a man who does not understand when a familiar language is spoken, has no understanding at all, or a very dull one. Moreover, I have said that if this being is understood, it is in the understanding. Is that in no understanding which has been proved necessarily to exist in the reality of fact?

But you will say that although it is in the understanding, it does not follow that it is understood. But observe that the fact of its being understood does necessitate its being in the understanding. For as what is conceived, is conceived by conception, and what is conceived by conception, as it is conceived, so is in conception; so what is understood, is understood by understanding, and what is understood by understanding, as it is understood, so is in the understanding. What can be more clear than this?

After this, I have said that if it is even in the understanding alone, it can be conceived also to exist in reality, which is greater. If, then, it is in the understanding alone, obviously the very being than which a greater cannot be conceived is one than which a greater can be conceived. What is more logical? For if it exists even in the understanding alone, can it not be conceived also to exist in reality? And if it can be so conceived, does not he who conceives of this conceive of a thing greater than that being, if it exists in the understanding alone? What more consistent inference, then, can be made than this: that if a being than which a greater cannot be conceived is in the understanding alone, it is not that than which a greater cannot be conceived?

But, assuredly, in no understanding is a being than which a greater is conceivable a being than which a greater is inconceivable. Does it not follow, then, that if a being than which a greater cannot be conceived is in any understanding, it does not exist in the understanding alone? For if it is in the understanding alone, it is a being than which a greater can be conceived, which is inconsistent with the hypothesis.

CHAPTER III.

A criticism of Gaunilo's example, in which he tries to show that in this way the real existence of a lost island might be inferred from the fact of its being conceived.

But, you say, it is as if one should suppose an island in the ocean, which surpasses all lands in its fertility, and which, because of the difficulty, or rather the impossibility, of discovering what does not exist, is called a lost island; and should say that there can be no doubt that this island truly exists in reality, for this reason, that one who hears it described easily understands what he hears.

Now I promise confidently that if any man shall devise anything existing either in reality or in concept alone (except that than which a greater cannot be conceived) to which he can adapt the sequence of my reasoning, I will discover that thing, and will give him his lost island, not to be lost again.

But it now appears that this being than which a greater is inconceivable cannot be conceived not to be, because it exists on so assured a ground of truth; for otherwise it would not exist at all.

Hence, if any one says that he conceives this being not to exist, I say that at the time when he conceives of this either he conceives of a being than which a greater is inconceivable, or he does not conceive at all. If he does not conceive, he does not conceive of the non-existence of that of which he does not conceive. But if he does conceive, he certainly conceives of a being which cannot be even conceived not to exist. For if it could be conceived not to exist, it could be conceived to have a beginning and an end. But this is impossible.

He, then, who conceives of this being conceives of a being which cannot be even conceived not to exist; but he who conceives of this being does not conceive that it does not exist; else he conceives what is inconceivable. The non-existence, then, of that than which a greater cannot be conceived is inconceivable.

CHAPTER IV.

The difference between the possibility of conceiving of non-existence, and understanding non-existence.

You say, moreover, that whereas I assert that this supreme being cannot be *conceived* not to exist, it might better be said that its non-existence, or even the possibility of its non-existence, cannot be *understood.*

But it was more proper to say, it cannot be conceived. For if I had said that the object itself cannot be understood not to exist, possibly you yourself, who say that in accordance with the true meaning of the term what is unreal cannot be understood, would offer the objection that nothing which is can be understood not to be, for the non-existence of what exists is unreal: hence God would not be the only being of which it could be said, it is impossible to understand its non-existence. For thus one of those beings which most certainly exist can be understood not to exist in the same way in which certain other real objects can be understood not to exist.

But this objection, assuredly, cannot be urged against the term *conception,* if one considers the matter well. For although no objects which exist can be understood not to exist, yet all objects, except that which exists in the highest degree, can be conceived not to exist. For all those objects, and those alone, can be conceived not to exist, which have a beginning or end or composition of parts: also, as I have already said, whatever at any place or at any time does not exist as a whole.

That being alone, on the other hand, cannot be conceived not to exist, in which any conception discovers neither beginning nor end nor composition of parts, and which any conception finds always and everywhere as a whole.

Be assured, then, that you can conceive of your own non-existence, although you are most certain that you exist. I am surprised that you should have admitted that you are ignorant of this. For we conceive of the non-existence of many objects which we know to exist, and of the existence of many which we know not to exist; not by forming the opinion that they so exist, but by imagining that they exist as we conceive of them.

And indeed, we can conceive of the non-existence of an object, although we know it to exist, because at the same time we can conceive of the former and know the latter. And we cannot conceive of the non-existence of an object, so long as we know it to exist, because we cannot conceive at the same time of existence and non-existence.

If, then, one will thus distinguish these two senses of this statement, he will understand that nothing, so long as it is known to exist, can be conceived not to exist; and that whatever exists, except that being than which a greater cannot be conceived, can be conceived not to exist, even when it is known to exist.

So, then, of God alone it can be said that it is impossible to conceive of his non-existence; and yet many objects, so long as they exist, in one sense cannot be conceived not to exist. But in what sense God is to be conceived not to exist, I think has been shown clearly enough in my book.

CHAPTER V.

A particular discussion of certain statements of Gaunilo's. In the first place, he misquoted the argument which he undertook to refute.

The nature of the other objections which you, in behalf of the fool, urge against me it is easy, even for a man of small wisdom, to detect; and I had therefore thought it unnecessary to show this. But since I hear that some readers of these objections think they have some weight against me, I will discuss them briefly.

In the first place, you often repeat that I assert that what is greater than all other beings is in the understanding; and if it is in the understanding, it exists also in reality, for otherwise the being which is greater than all would not be greater than all.

Nowhere in all my writings is such a demonstration found. For the real existence of a being which is said to be *greater than all other beings* cannot be demonstrated in the same way with the real existence of one that is said to be *a being than which a greater cannot be conceived*.

If it should be said that a being than which a greater cannot be conceived has no real existence, or that it is possible that it does not exist, or even that it can be conceived not to exist, such an assertion can be easily refuted. For the non-existence of what does not exist is possible, and that whose non-existence is possible can be conceived not to exist. But whatever can be conceived not to exist, if it exists, is not a being than which a greater cannot be conceived; but if it does not exist, it would not, even if it existed, be a being than which a greater cannot be conceived. But it cannot be said that a being than which a greater is inconceivable, if it exists, is not a being than which a greater is inconceivable; or that if it existed, it would not be a being than which a greater is inconceivable.

It is evident, then, that neither is it non-existent, nor is it possible that it does not exist, nor can it be conceived not to exist. For otherwise, if it exists, it is not that which it is said to be in the hypothesis; and if it existed, it would not be what it is said to be in the hypothesis.

But this, it appears, cannot be so easily proved of a being which is said to be *greater than all other beings*. For it is not so evident that what can be conceived not to exist is not greater than all existing beings, as it is evident that it is not a being than which a greater cannot be conceived. Nor is it so indubitable that if a being greater than all other beings exists, it is no other than the being than which a greater cannot be conceived; or that if it were such a being, some other might not be this being in like manner; as it is certain with regard to a being which is hypothetically posited as one than which a greater cannot be conceived.

For consider: if one should say that there is a being greater than all other beings, and that this being can nevertheless be conceived not to exist; and that a being greater than this, although it does not exist, can be conceived to exist: can it be so clearly inferred in this case that this being is therefore not a being greater than all other existing beings, as it would be most positively affirmed in the other case, that the being under discussion is not, therefore, a being than which a greater cannot be conceived?

For the former conclusion requires another premise than the predication, *greater than all other beings*. In my argument, on the other hand, there is no need of any other than this very predication, *a being than which a greater cannot be conceived*.

If the same proof cannot be applied when the being in question is predicated to be greater than all others, which can be applied when it is predicated to be a being than which a greater cannot be conceived, you have unjustly censured me for saying what I did not say; since such a predication differs so greatly from that which I actually made. If, on the other hand, the other argument is valid, you ought not to blame me for having said what can be proved.

Whether this can be proved, however, he will easily decide who recognises that this being than which a greater cannot be conceived is demonstrable. For by no means can this being than which a greater cannot be conceived be understood as any other than that which alone is greater than all. Hence, just as that than which a greater cannot be conceived is understood, and is in the understanding, and for that reason is asserted to exist in the reality of fact: so what is said to be greater than all other beings is understood and is in the understanding, and therefore it is necessarily inferred that it exists in reality.

You see, then, with how much justice you have compared me with your fool, who, on the sole ground that he understands what is described to him, would affirm that a lost island exists.

CHAPTER VI.

A discussion of Gaunilo's argument in his second chapter: that any unreal beings can be understood in the same way, and would, to that extent, exist.

Another of your objections is that any unreal beings, or beings whose existence is uncertain, can be understood and be in the understanding in the same way with that being which I discussed. I am surprised that you should have conceived this objection, for I was attempting to prove what was still uncertain, and contented myself at first with showing that this being is understood in any way, and is in the understanding. It was my intention to consider, on these grounds, whether this being is in the understanding alone, like an unreal object, or whether it also exists in fact, as a real being. For if unreal objects, or objects whose existence is uncertain, in this way are understood and are in the understanding, because, when they are spoken of, the hearer understands what the speaker means, there is no reason why that being of which I spoke should not be understood and be in the understanding.

How, moreover, can these two statements of yours be reconciled: (1) the assertion that if a man should speak of any unreal objects, whatever they might be, you would understand, and (2) the assertion that on hearing of that being which does exist, and not in that way in which even unreal objects are held in concept, you would not say that you conceive of it or have it in concept; since, as you say, you cannot conceive of it in any other way than by understanding it, that is, by comprehending in your knowledge its real existence?

How, I ask, can these two things be reconciled: that unreal objects are understood, and that understanding an object is comprehending in knowledge its real existence? The contradiction does not concern me: do you see to it. But if unreal objects are also in some sort understood, and your definition is applicable, not to every understanding, but to a certain sort of understanding, I ought not to be blamed for saying that a being than which a greater cannot be conceived is understood and is in the understanding, even before I reached the certain conclusion that this being exists in reality.

CHAPTER VII.

In answer to another objection: that the supremely great being may be conceived not to exist, just as by the fool God is conceived not to exist.

Again, you say that it can probably never be believed that this being, when it is spoken of and heard of, cannot be conceived not to exist in the same way in which even God may be conceived not to exist.

Such an objection could be answered by those who have attained but little skill in disputation and argument. For is it compatible with reason for a man to deny the existence of what he understands, because it is said to be that being whose existence he denies because he does not understand it? Or, if at some times its existence is denied, because only to a certain extent is it understood, and that which is not at all understood is the same to him: is not what is still undetermined more easily proved of a being which exists in some understanding than of one which exists is no understanding?

Hence it cannot be credible that any man denies the existence of a being than which a greater cannot be conceived, which, when he hears of it, he understands in a certain degree: it is incredible, I say, that any man denies the existence of this being because he denies the existence of God, the sensory perception of whom he in no wise conceives of.

Or if the existence of another object, because it is not at all understood, is denied, yet is not the existence of what is understood in some degree more easily proved than the existence of an object which is in no wise understood?

Not irrationally, then, has the hypothesis of a being a greater than which cannot be conceived been employed in controverting the fool, for the proof of the existence of God: since in some degree he would understand such a being, but in no wise could he understand God.

CHAPTER VIII.

The example of the picture, treated in Gaunilo's third chapter, is examined.—From what source a notion may be formed of the supremely great being, of which Gaunilo inquired in his fourth chapter.

Moreover, your so careful demonstration that the being than which a greater cannot be conceived is not analogous to the not yet executed picture in the understanding of the painter, is quite unnecessary. It was not for this purpose that I suggested the preconceived picture. I had no thought of asserting that the being which I was discussing is of such a nature; but I wished to show that what is not understood to exist can be in the understanding.

Again, you say that when you hear of a being than which a greater is inconceivable, you cannot conceive of it in terms of any real object known to you either specifically or generally, nor have it in your understanding. For, you say, you neither know such a being in itself, nor can you form an idea of it from anything like it.

But obviously this is not true. For everything that is less good, in so far as it is good, is like the greater good. It is therefore evident to any rational mind, that by ascending from the lesser good to the greater, we can form a considerable notion of a being than which a greater is inconceivable.

For instance, who (even if he does not believe that what he conceives of exists in reality) supposing that there is some good which has a beginning and an end, does not conceive that a good is much better, which, if it begins, does not cease to be? And that as the second good is better than the first, so that good which has neither beginning nor end, though it is ever passing from the past through the present to the future, is better than the second? And that far better than this is a being—whether any being of such a nature exists or not—which in no wise requires change or motion, nor is compelled to undergo change or motion?

Is this inconceivable, or is some being greater than this conceivable? Or is not this to form a notion from objects than which a greater is conceivable, of the being than which a greater cannot be conceived? There is, then, a means of forming a notion of a being than which a greater is inconceivable.

So easily, then, can the fool who does not accept sacred authority be refuted, if he denies that a notion may be formed from other objects of a being than which a greater is inconceivable. But if any Catholic would deny this, let him remember that the invisible things of God, from the creation of the world, are clearly seen, being understood by the things that are made, even his eternal power and Godhead. (Romans i. 20.)

CHAPTER IX.

The possibility of understanding and conceiving of the supremely great being. The argument advanced against the fool is confirmed.

But even if it were true that a being than which a greater is inconceivable cannot be conceived or understood; yet it would not be untrue that a being than which a greater cannot be conceived is conceivable and intelligible. There is nothing to prevent one's saying *ineffable*, although what is said to be ineffable cannot be spoken of. *Inconceivable* is conceivable, although that to which the word *inconceivable* can be applied is not conceivable. So, when one says, *that than which nothing greater is conceivable*, undoubtedly what is heard is conceivable and intelligible, although that being itself, than which a greater is inconceivable, cannot be conceived or understood.

Or, though there is a man so foolish as to say that there is no being than which a greater is inconceivable, he will not be so shameless as to say that he cannot understand or conceive of what he says. Or, if such a man is found, not only ought his words to be rejected, but he himself should be contemned.

Whoever, then, denies the existence of a being than which a greater cannot be conceived, at least understands and conceives of the denial which he makes. But this denial he cannot understand or conceive of without its component terms; and a term of this statement is *a being than which a greater cannot be conceived*. Whoever, then, makes this denial, understands and conceives of that than which a greater is inconceivable.

Moreover, it is evident that in the same way it is possible to conceive of and understand a being whose non-existence is impossible; but he who conceives of this conceives of a greater being than one whose non-existence is possible. Hence, when a being than which a greater is inconceivable is conceived, if it is a being whose non-existence is possible that is conceived, it is not a being than which a greater cannot be conceived. But an object cannot be at once conceived and not conceived. Hence he who conceives of a being than which a greater is inconceivable, does not conceive of that whose non-existence is possible, but of that whose non-existence is impossible. Therefore, what he conceives of must exist; for anything whose non-existence is possible, is not that of which he conceives.

CHAPTER X.

The certainty of the foregoing argument.—The conclusion of the book.

I believe that I have shown by an argument which is not weak, but sufficiently cogent, that in my former book I proved the real existence of a being than which a greater cannot be conceived; and I believe that this argument cannot be invalidated by the validity of any objection. For so great force does the signification of this reasoning contain in itself, that this being which is the subject of discussion, is of necessity, from the very fact that it is understood or conceived, proved also to exist in reality, and to be whatever we should believe of the divine substance.

For we attribute to the divine substance anything of which it can be conceived that it is better to be than not to be that thing. For example: it is better to be eternal than not eternal; good, than not good; nay, goodness itself, than not goodness itself. But it cannot be that anything of this nature is not a property of the being than which a greater is inconceivable. Hence, the being than which a greater is inconceivable must be whatever should be attributed to the divine essence.

I thank you for your kindness both in your blame and in your praise for my book. For since you have commended so generously those parts of it which seem to you worthy of acceptance, it is quite evident that you have criticised in no unkind spirit those parts of it which seemed to you weak.

2. ST. THOMAS AQUINAS (1225–1274)

[St. Thomas derived his philosophical inspiration primarily from Aristotle rather than Plato, and in keeping with
Aristotle's approach sought to base his own arguments
for God's existence upon certain facts of creation that any
man could observe. He nevertheless maintained, in keeping
with the Christian theological tradition, that God is a necessary being, or one whose non-existence is impossible,
and this, of course, comes very close to St. Anselm's claim
that no one having a true idea of God can rationally conceive of Him as non-existent. St. Thomas, however, felt
that no argument for God's existence could be derived from
this, for it would have the effect of proving that God's
existence is "self-evident," which it manifestly is not, or at
least, not to men.]

THOMAS' STATEMENT OF THE
ONTOLOGICAL ARGUMENT*

. . . [T]hose things are said to be self-evident which are
known as soon as the terms are known, which the Philosopher (I Poster. iii) says is true of the first principles of
demonstration. Thus, when the nature of a whole and of a
part is known, it is at once recognized that every whole is
greater than its part. But as soon as the signification of the
word "God" is understood, it is at once seen that God
exists. For by this word is signified that thing than which

* From the *Summa Theologica*, translated by the Fathers of
the English Dominican Province. Reprinted by permission of
the publishers: Burns & Oates, Ltd., London, and Benziger
Brothers, Inc., New York, copyright holders.

nothing greater can be conceived. But that which exists actually and mentally is greater than that which exists only mentally. Therefore, since as soon as the word "God" is understood it exists mentally, it also follows that it exists actually. Therefore the proposition "God exists" is self-evident.

HIS REPLY TO IT

Perhaps not everyone who hears this word "God" understands it to signify something than which nothing greater can be thought, seeing that some have believed God to be a body. Yet, granted that everyone understands that by this word "God" is signified something than which nothing greater can be thought, nevertheless, it does not therefore follow that he understands that what the word signifies exists actually, but only that it exists mentally. Nor can it be argued that it actually exists, unless it be admitted that there actually exists something than which nothing greater can be thought; and this precisely is not admitted by those who hold that God does not exist.

FURTHER COMMENT

A thing can be self-evident in either of two ways; on the one hand, self-evident in itself, though not to us; on the other, self-evident in itself, and to us. A proposition is self-evident because the predicate is included in the essence of the subject, as "Man is an animal," for animal is contained in the essence of man. If, therefore the essence of the predicate and subject be known to all, the proposition will be self-evident to all; as is clear with regard to the first principles of demonstration, the terms of which are common things that no one is ignorant of, such as being and nonbeing, whole and part, and suchlike. If, however, there are some to whom the essence of the predicate and subject is unknown, the proposition will be self-evident in itself, but not to those who do not know the meaning of the predicate and subject of the proposition. Therefore, it happens, as Boethius says (*Hebdom., the title of which is: "Whether all that is, is good"*), "that there are some mental concepts self-evident only to the learned, as that incorporeal substances are not in space." Therefore I say that this proposition, "God exists," of itself is self-evident, for the predicate is the same as the subject; because God is His own existence as will be hereafter shown (Q. III., A. 4). Now because we do not know the essence of God, the proposition is not self-evident to us; but needs to be demonstrated by things that are more known to us, though less known in their nature—namely, by effects.

3. RENÉ DESCARTES (1596–1650)

[*Descartes, who is thought of today as the founder of modern philosophy, did more to quicken interest in St. Anselm's idea than anyone up to that time, though he presented the argument as being of his own discovery. Such an argument was, in fact, most harmonious with his philosophical approach, and it is quite possible that St. Anselm's Proslogion was unknown to him when he composed his own argument. In matters of metaphysics, Descartes believed, one discovers truth by reason, which for him consisted in the pure analysis of ideas that are clearly and distinctly possessed. Whatever is a metaphysical truth is necessary or indubitable, and whatever is metaphysically false is impossible. Simply from the idea of God, therefore, Descartes thought that he could establish His existence with a metaphysical proof as rigorous as any proof found in mathematics.*]

A. DESCARTES' STATEMENT OF THE ONTOLOGICAL ARGUMENT*

If just because I can draw the idea of something from my thought, it follows that all which I know clearly and distinctly as pertaining to this object does really belong to it, may I not derive from this an argument demonstrating

* From Descartes' third *Meditation*, in *The Philosophical Works of Descartes*, Volume I, translated by Elizabeth S. Haldane and G. R. T. Ross. The remaining passages in this section are from Volume II of the same edition, and all are reprinted with the permission of the publisher, Cambridge University Press.

the existence of God? It is certain that I no less find the idea of God, that is to say, the idea of a supremely perfect Being, in me, than that of any figure or number whatever it is; and I do not know any less clearly and distinctly that an actual and eternal existence pertains to this nature than I know that all that which I am able to demonstrate of some figure or number truly pertains to the nature of this figure or number, and therefore, although all that I concluded in the preceding Meditations were found to be false, the existence of God would pass with me as at least as certain as I have ever held the truths of mathematics to be.

This indeed is not at first manifest, since it would seem to present some appearance of being a sophism. For being accustomed in all other things to make a distinction between existence and essence, I easily persuade myself that the existence can be separated from the essence of God, and that we can thus conceive God as not actually existing. But, nevertheless, when I think of it with more attention, I clearly see that existence can no more be separated from the essence of God than can its having its three angles equal to two right angles be separated from the essence of a rectilinear triangle, or the idea of a mountain from the idea of a valley; and so there is not any less repugnance to our conceiving a God (that is, a Being supremely perfect) to whom existence is lacking (that is to say, to whom a certain perfection is lacking), than to conceive of a mountain which has no valley.

But although I cannot really conceive of a God without existence any more than a mountain without a valley, still from the fact that I conceive of a mountain with a valley, it does not follow that there is such a mountain in the world; similarly although I conceive of God as possessing existence, it would seem that it does not follow that there is a God which exists; for my thought does not impose any necessity upon things, and just as I may imagine a winged horse, although no horse with wings exists, so I could perhaps attribute existence to God, although no God existed.

But a sophism is concealed in this objection; for from

the fact that I cannot conceive a mountain without a valley, it does not follow that there is any mountain or any valley in existence, but only that the mountain and the valley, whether they exist or do not exist, cannot in any way be separated one from the other. While from the fact that I cannot conceive God without existence, it follows that existence is inseparable from Him, and hence that He really exists; not that my thought can bring this to pass, or impose any necessity on things, but, on the contrary, because the necessity which lies in the thing itself, i.e. the necessity of the existence of God determines me to think in this way. For it is not within my power to think of God without existence (that is of a supremely perfect Being devoid of a supreme perfection) though it is in my power to imagine a horse either with wings or without wings.

And we must not here object that it is in truth necessary for me to assert that God exists after having presupposed that He possesses every sort of perfection, since existence is one of these, but that as a matter of fact my original supposition was not necessary, just as it is not necessary to consider that all quadrilateral figures can be inscribed in the circle; for supposing I thought this, I should be constrained to admit that the rhombus might be inscribed in the circle since it is a quadrilateral figure, which, however, is manifestly false. We must not, I say, make any such allegations because although it is not necessary that I should at any time entertain the notion of God, nevertheless whenever it happens that I think of a first and a sovereign Being, and, so to speak, derive the idea of Him from the storehouse of my mind, it is necessary that I should attribute to Him every sort of perfection, although I do not get so far as to enumerate them all, or to apply my mind to each one in particular. And this necessity suffices to make me conclude (after having recognised that existence is a perfection) that this first and sovereign Being really exists; just as though it is not necessary for me ever to imagine any triangle, yet, whenever I wish to consider a rectilinear figure composed only of three angles, it is absolutely essential that I should attribute to it all those properties which serve to bring about the conclusion that its three angles are not greater than two right angles, even although I may not then be considering this point in particular. But when I consider which figures are capable of being inscribed in the circle, it is in no wise necessary that I should think that all quadrilateral figures are of this number; on the contrary, I cannot even pretend that this is the case, so long as I do not desire to accept anything which I cannot conceive clearly and distinctly. And in consequence there is a great difference between the false suppositions such as this, and the true ideas born within me, the first and principal of which is that of God. For really I discern in many ways that this idea is not something factitious, and depending solely on my thought, but that it is the image of a true and immutable nature; first of all, because I cannot conceive anything but God himself to whose essence existence necessarily pertains; in the second place because it is not possible for me to conceive two or more Gods in this same position; and, granted that there is one such God who now exists, I see clearly that it is necessary that He should have existed from all eternity, and that He must exist eternally; and finally, because I know an infinitude of other properties in God, none of which I can either diminish or change.

For the rest, whatever proof or argument I avail myself of, we must always return to the point that it is only those things which we conceive clearly and distinctly that have the power of persuading me entirely. And although amongst the matters which I conceive of in this way, some indeed are manifestly obvious to all, while others only manifest themselves to those who consider them closely and examine them attentively; still, after they have once been discovered, the latter are not esteemed as any less certain than the former. For example, in the case of every right-angled triangle, although it does not so manifestly appear that the square of the base is equal to the squares of the two other sides as that this base is opposite to the greatest angle; still, when this has once been apprehended, we are just as certain of its truth as of the truth of the other. And as regards God, if my mind were not preoccupied with prejudices, and if my thought did not find itself on all hands diverted by the continual pressure of sensible things, there would be nothing which I could know more immediately and more easily than Him. For is there anything more manifest than that there is a God, that is to say, a Supreme Being, to whose essence alone existence pertains?

B.   OBJECTION TO DESCARTES' ARGUMENT
BY CATERUS
(A PRIEST AND CONTEMPORARY OF DESCARTES)

Let us then concede that someone has a clear and distinct idea of a highest and most perfect being; what further conclusion do you draw? That this infinite being exists, and that so certainly that the existence of God should have certitude, at least for my mind, as great as that which mathematical truths have hitherto enjoyed. Hence there is no less contradiction in thinking of a God (that is of a being of the highest perfection) who lacks existence (a particular perfection) than in thinking of a hill which is not relative to a valley. The whole dispute hinges on this; he who gives way here must admit defeat. Since my opponent is the stronger combatant I should like for a little to avoid engaging him at close quarters in order that, fated as I am to lose, I may yet postpone what I cannot avoid.

Firstly then, though reason only and not authority is the arbiter in our discussion, yet, lest I be judged impertinent in gainsaying the contentions of such an illustrious philosopher, let me quote you what St. Thomas says; it is an objection he urges against his own doctrine:—*As soon as the intellect grasps the signification of the name God, it knows that God exists; for the meaning of His name is an object nothing greater than which can be conceived. Now that which exists in fact as well as in the mind is greater than what exists in the mind alone. Hence, since the name "God" being understood, God consequently exists in the mind, it follows that He really exists.*[1] This argument

[1] Pages 28–29 of this volume.

formally expressed becomes—God is a being, a greater than which cannot be conceived; but that, a greater than which cannot be conceived, includes its existence; hence God by His very name or notion includes His existence, and as a direct consequence can neither be conceived as being, nor can be, devoid of existence. But now, kindly tell me is not this M. Descartes' own proof? St. Thomas defines God thus:—*A being than which nothing greater can be conceived.* M. Descartes calls Him a being of extreme perfection; certainly nothing greater than this can be conceived. St. Thomas goes on to argue:—*That than which nothing greater can be conceived includes its existence;* otherwise a greater than it could be conceived, namely that which is conceived to contain its existence. Now does not M. Descartes bring up the same proposition as minor premise? "God is the most perfect being, the most perfect being comprises within itself its existence, for otherwise it would not have the highest perfection." St. Thomas's conclusion is:—*Therefore since God, His name being understood, exists in the understanding, He exists in reality.* That is to say, owing to the very fact that in the very concept of the essence of an entity, nothing greater than which can be conceived, existence is involved, it follows that that very entity exists. M. Descartes draws the same inference:—Yet, says he, owing to the fact that we cannot think of God as not existing, it follows that His existence is inseparable from Him, and hence that He in truth exists. But now let St. Thomas reply both to himself and to M. Descartes. *Granted that everyone and anyone knows that by the name God is understood that which has been asserted, to wit, a being than which nothing greater can be thought, yet it does not follow that he understands that the thing signified by the name exists in reality, but only that it exists in the apprehension of the understanding. Nor can it be proved that it really exists, unless it be conceded that something really exists than which nothing greater can be thought—a proposition not granted by those who deny the existence of God.*[2] This furnishes me with

_____

[2] Page 29 of this volume.

my reply, which will be brief:—Though it be conceded that an entity of the highest perfection implies its existence by its very name, yet it does not follow that that very existence is anything actual in the real world, but merely that the concept of existence is inseparably united with the concept of highest being. Hence you cannot infer that the existence of God is anything actual, unless you assume that that highest being actually exists; for then it will actually contain all its perfections, together with this perfection of real existence.

Pardon me, gentlemen, if now I plead fatigue; but here is something in a lighter vein. This complex *existent Lion* includes both *lion* and the mode *existence;* and includes them essentially, for if you take away either it will not be the same complex. But now, has not God from all eternity had clear and distinct knowledge of this composite object? Does not also the idea of this composite, in so far as it is composite, involve both its elements essentially? That is to say, does not its existence flow from the essence of this composite, *existent Lion?* Yet, I affirm, the distinct cognition of it which God possesses, that which he has from all eternity does not constrain either part of the complex to exist, unless you assume that the complex does exist; for then, indeed, it will imply all its essential perfections and hence also that of actual existence. Therefore, also, even though you have a distinct knowledge of a highest being, and granted that a being of supreme perfection includes existence in the concept of its essence, yet it does not follow that its existence is anything actual, unless on the hypothesis that that highest being does exist; for then indeed along with its other perfections it will in actuality include this, its existence, also. Hence the proof of the existence of this highest being must be drawn from some other source.

C. DESCARTES' REPLY TO CATERUS

My opponent here compares one of my arguments with another of St. Thomas's, so, as it were to force me to show

which of the two has the more force. This I seem to be
able to do with a good enough grace, because neither did
St. Thomas use that argument as his own, nor does he
draw the same conclusion from it; consequently there is
nothing here in which I am at variance with the Angelic
Doctor. He himself asked whether the existence of God is
in itself known to man, i.e. whether it is obvious to each
single individual; he denies this, and I along with him.
Now the argument to which he puts himself in opposition
can be thus propounded. *When we understand what it is
the word God signifies, we understand that it is that,
than which nothing greater can be conceived; but to exist
in reality as well as in the mind is greater than to exist in
the mind alone; hence, when the meaning of the word God
is understood, it is understood that God exists in fact as
well as in the understanding.* Here there is a manifest error
in the form of the argument; for the only conclusion to be
drawn is—hence, when we understand what the word God
means, we understand that it means that God exists in
fact as well as in the mind: but because a word implies
something, that is no reason for this being true. My argument, however, was, of the following kind—That which we
clearly and distinctly understand to belong to the true and
immutable nature of anything, its essence, or form, can be
truly affirmed of that thing; but, after we have with
sufficient accuracy investigated the nature of God, we
clearly and distinctly understand that to exist belongs to
His true and immutable nature; therefore we can with
truth affirm of God that He exists. This is at least a
legitimate conclusion. But besides this the major premise
cannot be denied, because it was previously conceded that
whatever we clearly and distinctly perceive is true. The
minor alone remains, and in it there is, I confess, no little
difficulty. This is firstly because we are so much accustomed to distinguish existence from essence in the case of
other things, that we do not with sufficient readiness notice
how existence belongs to the essence of God in a greater
degree than in the case of other things. Further, because
we do not distinguish that which belongs to the true and
immutable nature of a thing from that which we by a

mental fiction assign to it, even if we do fairly clearly perceive that existence belongs to God's essence, we nevertheless do not conclude that God exists, because we do not know whether His essence is true and immutable or only a fiction we invent.

But, in order to remove the first part of this difficulty we must distinguish between possible and necessary existence, and note that in the concept or idea of everything that is clearly and distinctly conceived, possible existence is contained, but necessary existence never, except in the idea of God alone. For I am sure that all who diligently attend to this diversity between the idea of God and that of all other things, will perceive that, even though other things are indeed conceived only as existing, yet it does not thence follow that they do exist, but only that they may exist, because we do not conceive that there is any necessity for actual existence being conjoined with their other properties; but, because we understand that actual existence is necessarily and at all times linked to God's other attributes, it follows certainly that God exists.

Further, to clear away the rest of the difficulty, we must observe that those ideas which do not contain a true and immutable nature, but only a fictitious one due to a mental synthesis, can be by that same mind analysed, not merely by abstraction (or restriction of the thought) but by a clear and distinct mental operation; hence it will be clear that those things which the understanding cannot so analyse have not been put together by it. For example, when I think of a winged horse, or of a lion actually existing, or of a triangle inscribed in a square, I easily understand that I can on the contrary think of a horse without wings, of a lion as not existing and of a triangle apart from a square, and so forth, and that hence these things have no true and immutable nature. But if I think of the triangle or the square (I pass by for the present the lion and the horse, because their natures are not wholly intelligible to us), then certainly whatever I recognise as being contained in the idea of the triangle, as that its angles are equal to two right, etc., I shall truly affirm of the triangle; and similarly I shall affirm of the square whatsoever I find in the idea of it. For though I can think of the triangle, though stripping from it the equality of its angles to two right, yet I cannot deny that attribute of it by any clear and distinct mental operation, i.e. when I myself rightly understand what I say. Besides, if I think of a triangle inscribed in a square, not meaning to ascribe to the square that which belongs to the triangle alone, or to assign to the triangle the properties of the square, but for the purpose only of examining that which arises from the conjunction of the two, the nature of that composite will be not less true and immutable than that of the square or triangle alone; and hence it will be right to affirm that the square cannot be less than double the inscribed triangle, together with the similar properties which belong to the nature of this composite figure.

But if I think that existence is contained in the idea of a body of the highest perfection, because it is a greater perfection to exist in reality as well as in the mind than to exist in the intellect alone, I cannot then conclude that this utterly perfect body exists, but merely that it may exist; for I can well enough recognise that that idea has been put together by my mind uniting together all corporeal perfections, and that existence does not arise out of its other corporeal perfections, because it (existence) can be equally well affirmed and denied of them. Nay, because when I examine this idea of body I see in it no force by means of which it may produce or preserve itself, I rightly conclude that necessary existence, which alone is here in question, does not belong to the nature of a body, howsoever perfect it may be, any more than it belongs to the nature of a mountain not to have a valley, or any more than it pertains to the nature of a triangle to have its angles greater than two right angles. But now, if we ask not about a body but about a thing (of whatever sort this thing may turn out to be) which has all those perfections which can exist together, whether existence must be included in the number of these perfections we shall at first be in doubt, because our mind, being finite, and not accustomed to consider them unless separately, will perchance not at first see how necessary is the bond between them. But yet if we attentively consider whether existence is congruous with a being of the highest perfection, and what sort of existence is so, we shall be able clearly and distinctly to perceive in the first place that possible existence is at least predicable of it, as it is of all other things of which we have a distinct idea, even of those things which are composed by a fiction of the mind. Further, because we cannot think of God's existence as being possible, without at the same time, and by taking heed of His immeasurable power, acknowledging that He can exist by His own might, we hence conclude that He really exists and has existed from all eternity; for the light of nature makes it most plain that what can exist by its own power always exists. And thus we shall understand that necessary existence is comprised in the idea of a being of the highest power, not by any intellectual fiction, but because it belongs to the true and immutable nature of that being to exist. We shall at the same time easily perceive that that all-powerful being must comprise in himself all the other perfections that are contained in the idea of God, and hence these by their own nature and without any mental fiction are conjoined together and exist in God.

D. OBJECTION BY A GROUP OF SEVENTEENTH-CENTURY PHILOSOPHERS AND THEOLOGIANS

In your reply to the preceding set of objections you appear to have gone astray in the drawing of your conclusion. This was how you propounded your argument. *We may truly affirm of anything, that which we clearly and distinctly perceive to belong to its true and immutable nature; but (after we have investigated with sufficient accuracy what God is) we clearly and distinctly understand that to exist belongs to the nature of God.* The proper conclusion would have been:—*therefore (after we have investigated with sufficient accuracy what God is) we can truly affirm that to exist belongs to God's nature.* Whence it does not follow that God actually exists, but only that He ought to exist if His nature were anything possible or not contradictory; that is to say, that the nature or essence of God cannot be conceived apart from His existence and hence, as a consequence, if that essence is real, God exists as an actual fact. All this may be reduced to that argument which is stated by others in the following terms:—*If it is not a contradiction that God exists, it is certain that He exists; but His existence is not a contradiction; hence, etc.* But a difficulty occurs in the minor premise, which states that God's existence is not a contradiction, since our critics either profess to doubt the truth of this or deny it. Moreover that little clause in your argument ("after we have sufficiently investigated the nature of God") assumes as true something that all do not believe; and you know that you yourself confess that you can apprehend the infinite only inadequately. The same thing must be said in the case of each and any of God's attributes; for, since everything in God is utterly infinite, what mind can comprehend the smallest fragment of what exists in God except in a manner that is utterly inadequate? How then can you have "investigated with sufficient clearness and distinctness what God is"?

E. DESCARTES' REPLY

At the point where you criticise the conclusion of a syllogism constructed by me, you yourselves seem to make a blunder in the form of the argument. In order to derive the conclusion you desire, you should have worded the major premise thus: *that which we clearly understand to belong to the nature of anything, can truthfully be asserted to belong to its nature;* and consequently nothing but an unprofitable tautology will be contained in it. But my major premise was as follows—*that which we clearly understand to belong to the nature of anything can truly be affirmed of that thing.* Thus, if to be an animal belongs to the nature of man it can be asserted that man is animal: if to have its three angles equal to two right angles belongs to the nature of the triangle, it can be asserted that the triangle has its three angles equal to two right angles:

if existence belongs to the nature of God, it can be affirmed that God exists, etc. But my minor premise was *yet existence does belong to the nature of God*. Whence it is evident that the conclusion must be drawn as I drew it: *hence it can be truly affirmed of God that He exists;* but not as you wish: *hence we can truthfully affirm that existence belongs to the nature of God.*

Thus, in order to make use of the exception that you append, you should have denied the major and said: *that which we clearly understand to belong to the nature of anything, cannot on that account be ascribed to it, unless the nature of that thing be possible, or not contradictory.* But notice, kindly, how little value this exception has. By *possible* either you mean, as all commonly do, whatever does not disagree with human thought; and in this sense it is manifest that the nature of God, as I have described it, is possible, because I have assigned nothing to it that we did not clearly and distinctly perceive ought to belong to it, and consequently it cannot be in disagreement with our thought. Or surely you imagine some other kind of possibility, one proceeding from the object itself, but which, unless it agrees with the preceding variety can never be known by the human mind. But on this account it tells quite as much against everything else that man may know as against the nature or existence of God. For that which entitles us to deny that God's nature is possible though there is no impossibility on the part of its concept, (but on the contrary all the things included in that concept of the divine nature are so connected that there seems to be a contradiction in saying that any one of them does not belong to God), will permit us to deny that it is possible for the three angles of a triangle to be equal to two right angles, or that he, who actually thinks, exists. Much more right will there be to deny that anything we apprehend by our senses is true, and thus the whole of human knowledge will be overturned, though for no good reason.

To take the argument you compare with mine: if there is no contradiction in God's existence, it is certain that He exists; but there is no contradiction; therefore, etc., it is true materially though formally a sophism. For in the major premise the expression "there is contradiction" stands in relation to the concept of the cause by virtue of which God's existence is possible; but in the minor it applies merely to the concept of the divine nature and existence itself. As is evident; for if the major be denied the proof will have to go thus: if God has not yet existed, His existence is a contradiction, because no sufficient cause for bringing Him into existence can be assigned: but, as was assumed, His existence is not contradictory, hence, etc. If, on the other hand, the minor be denied, the proof must thus be stated: that is not contradictory in the formal concept of which there is nothing involving contradiction; but in the formal concept of the divine existence or nature there is nothing involving contradiction; therefore, etc. Now these two proofs are very diverse. For it is possible that in a certain thing nothing may be conceived that prevents the existence of that thing, though meanwhile on the side of the cause there is known to be something that opposes its coming into being.

But though we conceive God only inadequately, or, if you prefer to put it thus, in an utterly inadequate manner, this does not prevent its being certain that His nature is possible, or not contradictory; nor does it prevent our affirming truly that we have examined it with sufficient precision (i.e. with as much as is required in order to attain to this knowledge, and in order to know that necessary existence appertains to this same Divine nature). For all contradictoriness or impossibility is constituted by our thought, which cannot join together ideas that disagree with each other; it cannot reside in anything external to the mind, because by the very fact that a thing is outside the mind it is clear that it is not contradictory, but is possible. Moreover, contradictoriness in our concepts arises merely from their obscurity and confusion; there can be none in the case of clear and distinct ideas. Hence it suffices us to understand clearly and distinctly those few things that we perceive about God, though they form a quite inadequate knowledge, and to note that among the other constituents of this idea, however inadequate it be, necessary existence is found, in order to be able to affirm that we have examined the nature of God with sufficient precision, and to maintain that it contains no contradiction.

F. OBJECTION TO DESCARTES' ARGUMENT BY P. GASSENDI
(AN EMINENT CONTEMPORARY OF DESCARTES)

The vital part of your argument lies in these words: *When I think attentively I clearly see that the existence can no more be separated from the essence of God than can there be separated from the essence of a triangle the equality in magnitude of its three angles to two right angles, or the idea of a mountain from the idea of a valley; so that there is no less incongruity in our conceiving a God (i.e. a Being who is supremely perfect) to Whom existence is lacking (i.e. in Whom a certain perfection is missing), than to think of a mountain which is not accompanied by a valley.* But we must note that a comparison of this kind is not sufficiently accurate.

For though you properly enough compare essence with essence, in your next step it is neither existence with essence, nor property with property that you compare, but existence with property. Hence it seems that you either ought to have said that God's omnipotence can no more be separated from His essence than can that equality in magnitude of the angles of a triangle from its essence; or at least, that God's existence can no more be separated from His essence than the existence from the essence of a triangle. Thus taken, each comparison would have proceeded on correct lines, and the truth would have been conceded, not only of the former but of the latter, although this would not be evidence that you had established your conclusion that God necessarily exists, because neither does the triangle necessarily exist, although its essence and its existence cannot in reality be severed, howsoever much the mind separates them or thinks of them apart, in the same way as the Divine essence and existence may be thought of separately.

Next we must note that you place existence among the Divine perfections, without, however, putting it among the perfections of a triangle or of a mountain, though in exactly similar fashion, and in its own way, it may be said to be a perfection of each. But, sooth to say, existence is a perfection neither in God nor in anything else; it is rather that in the absence of which there is no perfection.

This must be so if, indeed, that which does not exist has neither perfection nor imperfection, and that which exists and has various perfections, does not have its existence as a particular perfection and as one of the number of its perfections, but as that by means of which the thing itself equally with its perfections is in existence, and without which neither can it be said to possess perfections, nor can perfections be said to be possessed by it. Hence neither is existence held to exist in a thing in the way that perfections do, nor if the thing lacks existence is it said to be imperfect (or deprived of a perfection), so much as to be nothing.

Wherefore, as in enumerating the perfections of a triangle you do not mention existence, nor hence conclude that the triangle exists, so, in enumerating the perfections of God, you ought not to have put existence among them, in order to draw the conclusion that God exists, unless you wanted to beg the question.

You say: *in everything else I have distinguished existence from essence but not in God.* But how, I pray, is the existence of Plato distinguished from the essence of Plato, unless by thought? For, supposing now that Plato no longer exists where is his essence? Is it not in the same way that essence and existence are distinguished by thought in God?

You yourself raise the objection: *Perhaps, just as from my thinking of a mountain with a valley, or of a winged horse, it does not follow that therefore either the mountain or such a horse exists; so from the fact that I think of God as existing it does not follow that He exists:* but you go on to argue that a sophism is latent here. But it would not be difficult to expose the fallacy which you have yourself constructed, especially by assuming something that is so manifest a contradiction as that an existing God does not exist, and not assuming the same thing about man, or horse.

But if you had drawn a parallel between the mountain with its valley, or the horse with its wings, and God as possessing knowledge, power and other attributes, then the difficulty would have been carried forward and you would have had to explain how it is possible for a sloping mountain or a winged horse to be thought of without their existing, while a God who has knowledge and power cannot be conceived of without His existence being involved.

You say: *that it is not in your power to think of God without existence* (*that is of a supremely perfect Being devoid of a supreme perfection*) *as it is within your power to imagine a horse either with wings or without wings.* But nothing is to be added to this, except that, as you are free to think of a horse that does not have wings without thinking of its existence, that existence which, if added, will be a perfection in it due to you; so you are free to think of a God that has knowledge, power and the other perfections, without thinking of His existence, which, if possessed by Him would render His perfection complete. Whence, just as from the fact that a horse is thought of as possessing the perfection of being winged, it is not therefore inferred that it has existence, the chief of perfections, through your instrumentality; so neither from the fact that God is considered as possessing knowledge and other perfections is His existence deduced from that: rather it finally remains to be proved. Although you say: *that existence quite as much as other perfections is included in the idea of a Being of the highest perfection,* you affirm what has to be proved, and assume your conclusion as a premiss. For I might also, on the other part, say that in the idea of a perfect Pegasus, there was contained not only the perfection of having wings, but also that of existing. For as God is thought to be perfect in every kind of perfection, so is Pegasus thought to be perfect in its own kind, and you can bring forward in criticism nothing which cannot, if the parallel between the two be duly observed, be taken to hold of both alike.

You say: *as in thinking of a triangle it is not necessary for me to think that its three angles are equal to two right angles, though that is none the less true, as is afterwards clear when we attend to the matter; so we may indeed think of the other perfections of God without thinking of His existence, though that is none the less true when we note that it is a perfection.* But you see what may be said, viz. that as that property is discovered afterwards to exist in the triangle, because a demonstration proves it, so we must employ a demonstration in order to discover existence in God. Otherwise it will certainly be easy for me to show that anything is in anything.

You say *that when you attribute all perfections to God, you do not act as if you imagined that all quadrilateral figures were inscribed in the circle; since, as herein you would err,—and this is borne out by your knowledge that the rhombus cannot be inscribed in it, you do not in the other case go astray, because you afterwards find that existence is congruent with God.* But this apparently, is inevitably to act in the same way; or, if that is not so, you must show that existence is not incompatible with God, in the same way as you prove that being inscribed in a circle is incompatible with the rhombus. I pass by your remaining assertions, which are either unexplained or unproved by you, or are solved by considerations you have already adduced.

G. DESCARTES' REPLY

Here I do not see to what class of reality you wish to assign existence, nor do I see why it may not be said to be a property as well as omnipotence, taking the word property as equivalent to any attribute or anything which can be predicated of a thing, as in the present case it should be by all means regarded. Nay, necessary existence in the case of God is also a true property in the strictest sense of the word, because it belongs to Him and forms part of His essence alone. Hence the existence of a triangle cannot be compared with the existence of God, because existence manifestly has a different relation to essence in the case of God and in the case of a triangle.

Nor is it more a begging of the question, to enumerate existence among the things belonging to the essence of God, than to reckon the equality of the three angles of a triangle to two right angles among the properties of the triangle.

Nor is it true that essence and existence can be thought, the one apart from the other in God, as in a triangle, because God is His existence, while a triangle is not its own existence. I do not, nevertheless, deny that existence is a possible perfection in the idea of a triangle, as it is a necessary one in the idea of God; for this fact makes the idea of the triangle one of higher rank than the ideas of those chimerical things whose existence can never be supposed. Hence you have not diminished the force of this argument of mine in the slightest, and you still remain deluded by that fallacy, which you say I could have exposed so easily.

You are plainly in error when you say that existence is not demonstrated of God, as it is demonstrated of the triangle that its three angles are equal to two right angles; for the way in which both are proved is alike, except that the demonstration proving existence in God is much simpler and clearer. I pass over the rest, because, though saying that I explain nothing, you yourself explain nothing and prove nothing, save only that you are able to prove nothing.

4. BENEDICT DE SPINOZA (1632–1677)

[*Spinoza, like Descartes, endeavored in his philosophy to emulate the rigor of mathematics, and his chief work, the* Ethics, *was actually composed as a series of demonstrations, analogous in every way to the* Elements *of Euclid. His proof of God's existence is not essentially different from that of Descartes, though formulated in different terms. He supposes God to be a being such that, if He exists at all, He exists by His very nature, not deriving His existence from anything external to Himself. God, thus conceived, cannot fail to exist and cannot be thought of as coming into existence or ever ceasing. Spinoza, however, identified God, conceived as a necessary and self-sufficient being, with "substance," that is to say, with reality itself, maintaining that whatever exists, exists only in God and can have no existence apart from God.*]

God,* or substance, consisting of infinite attributes, of which each expresses eternal and infinite essentiality, necessarily exists.

Proof.—If this be denied, conceive, if possible, that God does not exist: then his essence does not involve existence. But this (by Prop. vii.[1]) is absurd. Therefore God necessarily exists.

Another proof.—Of everything whatsoever a cause or reason must be assigned, either for its existence, or for its non-existence—*e.g.* if a triangle exist, a reason or cause

* From *Improvement of the Understanding, Ethics, and Correspondence of Benedict de Spinoza,* translated by R. H. M. Elwes (London: M. W. Dunne, 1901).

[1] Prop. vii: Existence belongs to the nature of substance.

must be granted for its existence; if, on the contrary, it does not exist, a cause must also be granted, which prevents it from existing, or annuls its existence. This reason or cause must either be contained in the nature of the thing in question, or be external to it. For instance, the reason for the non-existence of a square circle is indicated in its nature, namely, because it would involve a contradiction. On the other hand, the existence of substance follows also solely from its nature, inasmuch as its nature involves existence. (See Prop. vii.)

But the reason for the existence of a triangle or a circle does not follow from the nature of those figures, but from the order of universal nature in extension. From the latter it must follow, either that a triangle necessarily exists, or that it is impossible that it should exist. So much is self-evident. It follows therefrom that a thing necessarily exists, if no cause or reason be granted which prevents its existence.

If, then, no cause or reason can be given, which prevents the existence of God, or which destroys his existence, we must certainly conclude that he necessarily does exist. If such a reason or cause should be given, it must either be drawn from the very nature of God, or be external to him —that is, drawn from another substance of another nature. For if it were of the same nature, God, by that very fact, would be admitted to exist. But substance of another nature could have nothing in common with God (by Prop. ii.[2]), and therefore would be unable either to cause or to destroy his existence.

As, then, a reason or cause which would annul the divine existence cannot be drawn from anything external to the divine nature, such cause must perforce, if God does not exist, be drawn from God's own nature, which would involve a contradiction. To make such an affirmation about a being absolutely infinite and supremely perfect, is absurd; therefore, neither in the nature of God, nor externally to his nature, can a cause or reason be assigned

[2] Prop. ii: Two substances, whose attributes are different, have nothing in common.

which would annul his existence. Therefore, God necessarily exists. *Q.E.D.*

Another proof.—The potentiality of non-existence is a negation of power, and contrariwise the potentiality of existence is a power, as is obvious. If, then, that which necessarily exists is nothing but finite beings, such finite beings are more powerful than a being absolutely infinite, which is obviously absurd; therefore, either nothing exists, or else a being absolutely infinite necessarily exists also. Now we exist either in ourselves, or in something else which necessarily exists (see Axiom i.[3] and Prop. vii.). Therefore a being absolutely infinite—in other words, God (Def. vi.[4])—necessarily exists. *Q.E.D.*

Note.—In this last proof, I have purposely shown God's existence *à posteriori*, so that the proof might be more easily followed, not because, from the same premises, God's existence does not follow *à priori*. For, as the potentiality of existence is a power, it follows that, in proportion as reality increases in the nature of a thing, so also will it increase its strength for existence. Therefore a being absolutely infinite, such as God, has from himself an absolutely infinite power of existence, and hence he does absolutely exist. Perhaps there will be many who will be unable to see the force of this proof, inasmuch as they are accustomed only to consider those things which flow from external causes. Of such things, they see that those which quickly come to pass—that is, quickly come into existence—quickly also disappear; whereas they regard as more difficult of accomplishment—that is, not so easily brought into existence—those things which they conceive as more complicated.

However, to do away with this misconception, I need not here show the measure of truth in the proverb, "What comes quickly, goes quickly," nor discuss whether, from the point of view of universal nature, all things are equally

[3] Axiom i: Everything which exists, exists either in itself or in something else.

[4] Def. vi: By *God*, I mean a being absolutely infinite—that is, a substance consisting in infinite attributes, of which each expresses eternal and infinite essentiality.

easy, or otherwise: I need only remark, that I am not here speaking of things, which come to pass through causes external to themselves, but only of substances which (by Prop. vi.[5]) cannot be produced by any external cause. Things which are produced by external causes, whether they consist of many parts or few, owe whatsoever perfection or reality they possess solely to the efficacy of their external cause, and therefore their existence arises solely from the perfection of their external cause, not from their own. Contrariwise, whatsoever perfection is possessed by substance is due to no external cause; wherefore the existence of substance must arise solely from its own nature, which is nothing else but its essence. Thus, the perfection of a thing does not annul its existence, but, on the contrary, asserts it. Imperfection, on the other hand, does annul it; therefore we cannot be more certain of the existence of anything, than of the existence of a being absolutely infinite or perfect—that is, of God. For inasmuch as his essence excludes all imperfection, and involves absolute perfection, all cause for doubt concerning his existence is done away, and the utmost certainty on the question is given. This, I think, will be evident to every moderately attentive reader.

[5] Prop. vi: One substance cannot be produced by another substance.

5. GOTTFRIED WILHELM LEIBNIZ
(1646–1716)

[*Leibniz considered the Cartesian form of the argument to be valid, but incomplete, inasmuch as it presupposed the possibility of that which it purported to prove. If the supreme being, as conceived by Descartes, should be one that could not exist in reality, then no purely formal proof could establish its necessary existence. Leibniz, accordingly, proposed to show first that it is possible for such a being to exist, given which it follows, from the ontological argument, that God does exist.*]

Although* I am for innate ideas, and in particular for that of God, I do not think that the demonstration of the Cartesians drawn from the idea of God are perfect. I have shown fully elsewhere (in the "Actes de Leipsic," and in the "Memoires de Trevoux") that what Descartes has borrowed from Anselm, Archbishop of Canterbury, is very beautiful and really very ingenious, but that there is still a gap therein to be filled. This celebrated archbishop, who was without doubt one of the most able men of his time, congratulates himself, not without reason, for having discovered a means of proving the existence of God *a priori*, by means of its own notion, without recurring to its effects. And this is very nearly the force of his argument: God is the greatest or (as Descartes says) the most perfect of beings, or rather a being of supreme grandeur and per-

* From *The New Essays Concerning Human Understanding*, translated by A. G. Langley, 3rd edition, 1949. This and the following selection are reprinted by permission of The Open Court Publishing Company.

fection, including all degrees thereof. That is the notion of God. See now how existence follows from this notion. To exist is something more than not to exist, or rather, existence adds a degree to grandeur and perfection, and as Descartes states it, existence is itself a perfection. Therefore this degree of grandeur and perfection, or rather this perfection which consists in existence, is in this supreme all-great, all-perfect being: for otherwise some degree would be wanting to it, contrary to its definition. Consequently this supreme being exists. The Scholastics, not excepting even their Doctor Angelicus, have misunderstood this argument, and have taken it as a paralogism; in which respect they were altogether wrong, and Descartes, who studied quite a long time the scholastic philosophy at the Jesuit College of La Fleche, had great reason for reestablishing it. It is not a paralogism, but it is an imperfect demonstration, which assumes something that must still be proved in order to render it mathematically evident; that is, it is tacitly assumed that this idea of the all-great or all-perfect being is possible, and implies no contradiction. And it is already something that by this remark it is proved that, *assuming that God is possible, he exists,* which is the privilege of divinity alone. We have the right to presume the possibility of every being, and especially that of God, until some one proves the contrary. So that this metaphysical argument already gives a morally demonstrative conclusion, which declares that according to the present state of our knowledge we must judge that God exists, and act in conformity thereto. But it is to be desired, nevertheless, that clever men achieve the demonstration with the strictness of a mathematical proof, and I think I have elsewhere said something that may serve this end.

THAT THE MOST PERFECT BEING EXISTS[1]

I call every simple quality which is positive and absolute, or expresses whatever it expresses without any limits, a *perfection.*

[1] Here Leibniz proposes to demonstrate that the idea of God is a *logically consistent* idea, i.e., that God is *possible.*

But a quality of this sort, because it is simple, is therefore irresolvable or indefinable, for otherwise, either it will not be a simple quality but an aggregate of many, or, if it is one, it will be circumscribed by limits and so be known through negations of further progress contrary to the hypothesis, for a purely positive quality was assumed.

From these considerations it is not difficult to show that *all perfections are compatible with each other* or can exist in the same subject.

For let the proposition be of this kind:

A and B are incompatible

(for understanding by A and B two simple forms of this kind or perfections, and it is the same if more are assumed like them), it is evident that it cannot be demonstrated without the resolution of the terms A and B, of each or both; for otherwise their nature would not enter into the ratiocination and the incompatibility could be demonstrated as well from any others as from themselves. But now (by hypothesis) they are irresolvable. Therefore this proposition cannot be demonstrated from these forms.

But it might certainly be demonstrated by these if it were true, because it is not true *per se*, for all propositions necessarily true are either demonstrable or known *per se*. Therefore, this proposition is not necessarily true.

It is granted, therefore, that either a subject of all perfections or the most perfect being can be known.

Whence it is evident that it also exists, since existence is contained in the number of the perfections.

I showed this reasoning to D. Spinoza when I was in The Hague, who thought it solid; for when at first he opposed it, I put it in writing and read this paper before him.

6. IMMANUEL KANT (1724–1804)

[*It was mainly Kant's extensive criticism of the ontological argument that gave currency to the dictum that "existence is not a predicate," though essentially the same criticism had been anticipated by Gaunilo, and rejected by St. Anselm as irrelevant to his argument. Believing, perhaps rightly, that Descartes had treated existence as a "perfection," and therefore as a "predicate" or property of God, Kant argued, in effect, that the existence of a thing is presupposed in its having any properties at all and cannot, therefore, itself be considered a property of anything. This issue has been extensively debated in philosophy since Kant's time, quite independently of the ontological argument.*]

THE IMPOSSIBILITY OF AN ONTOLOGICAL PROOF OF THE EXISTENCE OF GOD*

In all ages men have spoken of an absolutely necessary being, and in so doing have endeavoured, not so much to understand whether and how a thing of this kind allows even of being thought, but rather to prove its existence. There is, of course, no difficulty in giving a verbal definition of the concept, namely, that it is something the non-existence of which is impossible. But this yields no insight into the conditions which make it necessary to regard the non-existence of a thing as absolutely unthinkable. It is

*From *The Critique of Pure Reason*, translated by Norman Kemp Smith, 1929. Reprinted by permission of the publishers: Macmillan & Company, Ltd., London, and St. Martin's Press, Inc., New York.

precisely these conditions that we desire to know, in order that we may determine whether or not, in resorting to this concept, we are thinking anything at all. The expedient of removing all those conditions which the understanding indispensably requires in order to regard something as necessary, simply through the introduction of the word unconditioned, is very far from sufficing to show whether I am still thinking anything in the concept of the unconditionally necessary, or perhaps rather nothing at all.

Nay more, this concept, at first ventured upon blindly, and now become so completely familiar, has been supposed to have its meaning exhibited in a number of examples; and on this account all further enquiry into its intelligibility has seemed to be quite needless. Thus the fact that every geometrical proposition, as, for instance, that a triangle has three angles, is absolutely necessary, has been taken as justifying us in speaking of an object which lies entirely outside the sphere of our understanding as if we understood perfectly what it is that we intend to convey by the concept of that object.

All the alleged examples are, without exception, taken from judgments, not from things and their existence. But the unconditioned necessity of judgments is not the same as an absolute necessity of things. The absolute necessity of the judgment is only a conditional necessity of the thing, or of the predicate in the judgment. The above proposition does not declare that three angles are absolutely necessary, but that, under the condition that there is a triangle (that is, that a triangle is given), three angles will necessarily be found in it. So great, indeed, is the deluding influence exercised by this logical necessity that, by the simple device of forming an *a priori* concept of a thing in such a manner as to include existence within the scope of its meaning, we have supposed ourselves to have justified the conclusion that because existence necessarily belongs to the object of this concept—always under the condition that we posit the thing as given (as existing)— we are also of necessity, in accordance with the law of identity, required to posit the existence of its object, and that this being is therefore itself absolutely necessary—and this, to repeat, for the reason that the existence of this being has already been thought in a concept which is assumed arbitrarily and on condition that we posit its object.

If, in an identical proposition, I reject the predicate while retaining the subject, contradiction results; and I therefore say that the former belongs necessarily to the latter. But if we reject subject and predicate alike, there is no contradiction; for nothing is then left that can be contradicted. To posit a triangle, and yet to reject its three angles, is self-contradictory; but there is no contradiction in rejecting the triangle together with its three angles. The same holds true of the concept of an absolutely necessary being. If its existence is rejected, we reject the thing itself with all its predicates; and no question of contradiction can then arise. There is nothing outside it that would then be contradicted, since the necessity of the thing is not supposed to be derived from anything external; nor is there anything internal that would be contradicted, since in rejecting the thing itself we have at the same time rejected all its internal properties. "God is omnipotent" is a necessary judgment. The omnipotence cannot be rejected if we posit a Deity, that is, an infinite being; for the two concepts are identical. But if we say, "There is no God," neither the omnipotence nor any other of its predicates is given; they are one and all rejected together with the subject, and there is therefore not the least contradiction in such a judgment.

We have thus seen that if the predicate of a judgment is rejected together with the subject, no internal contradiction can result, and that this holds no matter what the predicate may be. The only way of evading this conclusion is to argue that there are subjects which cannot be removed, and must always remain. That, however, would only be another way of saying that there are absolutely necessary subjects; and that is the very assumption which I have called in question, and the possibility of which the above argument professes to establish. For I cannot form the least concept of a thing which, should it be rejected with all its predicates, leaves behind a contradiction; and in the absence of contradiction I have, through pure *a priori* concepts alone, no criterion of impossibility.

Notwithstanding all these general considerations, in which every one must concur, we may be challenged with a case which is brought forward as proof that in actual fact the contrary holds, namely, that there is one concept, and indeed only one, in reference to which the not-being or rejection of its object is in itself contradictory, namely, the concept of the *ens realissimum*. It is declared that it possesses all reality, and that we are justified in assuming that such a being is possible (the fact that a concept does not contradict itself by no means proves the possibility of its object: but the contrary assertion I am for the moment willing to allow). Now [the argument proceeds] "all reality" includes existence; existence is therefore contained in the concept of a thing that is possible. If, then, this thing is rejected, the internal possibility of the thing is rejected—which is self-contradictory.

My answer is as follows. There is already a contradiction in introducing the concept of existence—no matter under what title it may be disguised—into the concept of a thing which we profess to be thinking solely in reference to its possibility. If that be allowed as legitimate, a seeming victory has been won; but in actual fact nothing at all is said: the assertion is a mere tautology. We must ask: Is the proposition that *this or that thing* (which, whatever it may be, is allowed as possible) *exists*, an analytic or a synthetic proposition? If it is analytic the assertion of the existence of the thing adds nothing to the thought of the thing; but in that case either the thought, which is in us, is the thing itself, or we have presupposed an existence as belonging to the realm of the possible, and have then, on that pretext, inferred its existence from its internal possibility—which is nothing but a miserable tautology. The word "reality," which in the concept of the thing sounds other than the word "existence" in the concept of the predicate, is of no avail in meeting this objection. For if all positing (no matter what it may be that is posited) is entitled reality, the thing with all its predicates is already posited in the concept of the subject, and is assumed as actual; and in the predicate this is merely repeated. But if, on the other hand, we admit, as every reasonable person must, that all existential propositions are synthetic, how can we profess to maintain that the predicate of existence cannot be rejected without contradiction? This is a feature which is found only in analytic propositions, and is indeed precisely what constitutes their analytic character.

I should have hoped to put an end to these idle and fruitless disputations in a direct manner, by an accurate determination of the concept of existence, had I not found that the illusion which is caused by the confusion of a logical with a real predicate (that is, with a predicate which determines a thing) is almost beyond correction. Anything we please can be made to serve as a logical predicate; the subject can even be predicated of itself; for logic abstracts from all content. But a determining predicate is a predicate which is added to the concept of the subject and enlarges it. Consequently, it must not be already contained in the concept.

"Being" is obviously not a real predicate; that is, it is not a concept of something which could be added to the concept of a thing. It is merely the positing of a thing, or of certain determinations, as existing in themselves. Logically, it is merely the copula of a judgment. The proposition, "God is omnipotent," contains two concepts, each of which has its object—God and omnipotence. The small word "is" adds no new predicate, but only serves to posit the predicate *in its relation* to the subject. If, now, we take the subject (God) with all its predicates (among which is omnipotence), and say "God is," or "There is a God," we attach no new predicate to the concept of God, but only posit the subject in itself with all its predicates, and indeed posit it as being an *object* that stands in relation to my *concept*. The content of both must be one and the same; nothing can have been added to the concept, which expresses merely what is possible, by my thinking its object (through the expression "it is") as given absolutely. Otherwise stated, the real contains no more than the merely possible. A hundred real thalers do not contain the least coin more than a hundred possible thalers. For as the latter

signify the concept, and the former the object and the positing of the object, should the former contain more than the latter, my concept would not, in that case, express the whole object, and would not therefore be an adequate concept of it. My financial position is, however, affected very differently by a hundred real thalers than it is by the mere concept of them (that is, of their possibility). For the object, as it actually exists, is not analytically contained in my concept, but is added to my concept (which is a determination of my state) synthetically; and yet the conceived hundred thalers are not themselves in the least increased through thus acquiring existence outside my concept.

By whatever and by however many predicates we may think a thing—even if we completely determine it—we do not make the least addition to the thing when we further declare that this thing *is*. Otherwise, it would not be exactly the same thing that exists, but something more than we had thought in the concept; and we could not, therefore, say that the exact object of my concept exists. If we think in a thing every feature of reality except one, the missing reality is not added by my saying that this defective thing exists. On the contrary, it exists with the same defect with which I have thought it, since otherwise what exists would be something different from what I thought. When, therefore, I think a being as the supreme reality, without any defect, the question still remains whether it exists or not. For though, in my concept, nothing may be lacking of the possible real content of a thing in general, something is still lacking in its relation to my whole state of thought, namely, that knowledge of this object is also possible *a posteriori*. And here we find the source of our present difficulty. Were we dealing with an object of the senses, we could not confound the existence of the thing with the mere concept of it. For through the concept the object is thought only as conforming to the *universal conditions* of possible empirical knowledge in general, whereas through its existence it is thought as belonging to the context of experience as a whole. In being thus connected with the content of experience as a whole, the concept of the object is not, however, in the least enlarged; all that has happened is that our thought has thereby obtained an additional possible perception. It is not, therefore, surprising that, if we attempt to think existence through the pure category alone, we cannot specify a single mark distinguishing it from mere possibility.

Whatever, therefore, and however much, our concept of an object may contain, we must go outside it, if we are to ascribe existence to the object. In the case of objects of the senses, this takes place through their connection with some one of our perceptions, in accordance with empirical laws. But in dealing with objects of pure thought, we have no means whatsoever of knowing their existence, since it would have to be known in a completely *a priori* manner. Our consciousness of all existence (whether immediately through perception, or mediately through inferences which connect something with perception) belongs exclusively to the unity of experience; any [alleged] existence outside this field, while not indeed such as we can declare to be absolutely impossible, is of the nature of an assumption which we can never be in a position to justify.

The concept of a supreme being is in many respects a very useful idea; but just because it is a mere idea, it is altogether incapable, by itself alone, of enlarging our knowledge in regard to what exists. It is not even competent to enlighten us as to the *possibility* of any existence beyond that which is known in and through experience. The analytic criterion of possibility, as consisting in the principle that bare positives (realities) give rise to no contradiction, cannot be denied to it. But since the realities are not given to us in their specific characters; since even if they were, we should still not be in a position to pass judgment; since the criterion of the possibility of synthetic knowledge is never to be looked for save in experience, to which the object of an idea cannot belong, the connection of all real properties in a thing is a synthesis, the possibility of which we are unable to determine *a priori*. And thus the celebrated Leibniz is far from having succeeded in what he plumed himself on achieving—the comprehension *a priori* of the possibility of this sublime ideal being.

The attempt to establish the existence of a supreme being by means of the famous ontological argument of Descartes is therefore merely so much labour and effort lost; we can no more extend our stock of [theoretical] insight by mere ideas, than a merchant can better his position by adding a few noughts to his cash account.

7. ARTHUR SCHOPENHAUER (1788–1860)

[*Schopenhauer reiterated the central point in Kant's criticism, but in language that is more readily understandable. It is a common reaction to the ontological argument that it succeeds in "proving" its conclusion only by first concealing that conclusion somewhere in its premises, and in this respect Schopenhauer compared it to a sleight-of-hand trick, wherein what is produced for the astonishment and wonder of the audience has been before them all the while, though carefully concealed until the appropriate time.*]

We* find even the excellent Descartes, who gave the first impulse to subjective reflection and thereby became the father of modern philosophy, still entangled in confusions for which it is difficult to account; and we shall soon see to what serious and deplorable consequences these confusions have led with regard to Metaphysics. In the "*Responsio ad secundas objectiones in meditationes de prima philosophia,*" *axioma i.* he says: *Nulla res existit, de qua non possit quæri, quænam sit causa, cur existat. Hoc enim de ipso Deo quæri potest, non quod indigeat ulla causa ut existat, sea quia ipsa ejus naturæ immensitas est* CAUSA, SIVE RATIO, *propter quam nulla causa indiget ad existendum.*[1] He ought to have said: The immensity of

---

* From *The Fourfold Root of the Principle of Sufficient Reason*, translated by Mme. Karl Hillebrand, revised edition. London: George Bell and Sons, 1897 (first edition 1889).

[1] "Reply to the Second Set of Objections to the Meditations," Axiom I, he says: "Nothing exists concerning which it may not be asked what the cause of its existence is. This may be asked even of God; not that he needs any cause in order to exist, but

God is a logical reason from which it follows, that God needs no cause; whereas he confounds the two together and obviously has no clear consciousness of the difference between reason and cause. Properly speaking however, it is his intention which mars his insight. For here, where the law of causality demands a *cause*, he substitutes a *reason* instead of it, because the latter, unlike the former, does not immediately lead to something beyond it; and thus, by means of this very axiom, he clears the way to the *Ontological Proof* of the existence of God, which was really his invention, for Anselm had only indicated it in a general manner. Immediately after these axioms, of which I have just quoted the first, there comes a formal, quite serious statement of the Ontological Proof, which, in fact, already lies within that axiom, as the chicken does within the egg that has been long brooded over. Thus, while everything else stands in need of a cause for its existence, the immensity implied in the conception of the Deity—who is introduced to us upon the ladder of the Cosmological Proof—suffices in lieu of a cause or, as the proof itself expresses it: *in conceptu entis summe perfecti existentia necessaria continetur.*[2] This, then, is the sleight-of-hand trick, for the sake of which the confusion, familiar even to Aristotle, of the two principal meanings of the principle of sufficient reason, has been used directly *in majorem Dei gloriam.*

Considered by daylight, however, and without prejudice, this famous Ontological Proof is really a charming joke. On some occasion or other, some one excogitates a conception, composed out of all sorts of predicates, among which however he takes care to include the predicate actuality or existence, either openly stated or wrapped up for decency's sake in some other predicate, such as perfection, immensity, or something of the kind. Now, it is well known,—that, from a given conception, those predicates which are essential to it—*i.e.*, without which it cannot be

because the cause or reason, why he needs no cause in order to exist, is in the very immensity of his nature."

[2] "Necessary existence is contained in the concept of a supremely perfect being."

thought—and likewise the predicates which are essential to those predicates themselves, may be extracted by means of purely logical analyses, and consequently have *logical* truth: that is, they have their reason of knowledge in the given conception. Accordingly the predicate reality or existence is now extracted from this arbitrarily thought conception, and an object corresponding to it is forthwith presumed to have real existence independently of the conception.

> "Were not the thought so cursedly acute,
> One might be tempted to declare it silly."[3]

After all, the simplest answer to such ontological demonstrations is: "All depends upon the source whence you have derived your conception: if it be taken from experience, all well and good, for in this case its object exists and needs no further proof; if, on the contrary, it has been hatched in your own *sinciput,* all its predicates are of no avail, for it is a mere phantasm. But we form an unfavourable prejudice against the pretensions of a theology which needed to have recourse to such proofs as this in order to gain a footing on the territory of philosophy, to which it is quite foreign, but on which it longs to trespass. But oh! for the prophetic wisdom of Aristotle! He had never even heard of the Ontological Proof; yet as though he could detect this piece of scholastic jugglery through the shades of coming darkness and were anxious to bar the road to it, he carefully shows[4] that defining a thing and proving its existence are two different matters, separate to all eternity; since by the one we learn *what* it is that is meant, and by the other *that* such a thing exists. Like an oracle of the future, he pronounces the sentence: τὸ δ' εἶναι οὐκ οὐσία οὐδενί· οὐ γὰρ γένος τὸ ὄν: (ESSE *autem nullius rei essentia est, quandoquidem ens non est genus*) which means: "Existence never can belong to the essence of a thing."

---

[3] Schiller, "Wallenstein-Trilogie. Piccolomini," Act ii. Sc. 7.
[4] Aristotle, "Analyt. post." c. 7.

PART II

CONTEMPORARY VIEWS OF
THE ONTOLOGICAL ARGUMENT

8. G. E. MOORE (1873–1958)

[*One of the moving spirits of twentieth-century philosophy, G. E. Moore is noted for his unusually clear thinking and writing. In this essay Moore does not mention the ontological argument. However, he does offer a penetrating discussion of the claim—made by Kant and Schopenhauer in order to refute the ontological argument—that existence is not a predicate. What we must ask here, says Moore, is what it means to say either that existence is or that it is not a predicate. Moore's essay is a masterpiece of clarity and an extraordinarily acute contribution to the discussion.*]

IS EXISTENCE A PREDICATE?*

I am not at all clear as to the meaning of this question. Mr. Kneale says that existence is not a predicate. But what does he mean by the words "Existence is not a predicate"?

In his second paragraph, he says that the word "predicate" has two different senses, a logical sense and a grammatical one. If so, it would follow that the words "Existence is not a predicate" may have two different meanings, according as the person who uses them is using "predicate" in the logical or the grammatical sense. And I think it is clear that he means us to understand that when

* This essay was the second paper in a symposium originally published in the *Proceedings of the Aristotelian Society,* Supplementary Volume XV, 1936, and is reprinted by permission of the Editor of the Aristotelian Society. Mr. William Kneale was the author of the first paper in the symposium.

he says "Existence is not a predicate," he is using "predicate" in the logical sense, and not in the grammatical one.
I think his view is that if anyone were to say "Existence is
a predicate," using "predicate" in the grammatical sense,
such a person would be perfectly right: I think he holds
that existence really is a predicate in the grammatical
sense. But, whether he holds this or not, I think it is clear
that he does not wish to discuss the question whether it is
or is not a predicate in the grammatical sense, but solely
the question whether it is so in the logical one.

Now I think it is worth noticing that if we assert "Existence is a predicate," using "predicate" in the grammatical
sense, our proposition is a proposition about certain *words*,
to the effect that they are often used in a certain way; but
not, curiously enough, about the word "existence" itself. It is a proposition to the effect that the word "exists"
and other finite parts of the verb "to exist," such as
"existed," "will exist," or "exist" (in the plural) are often
the predicates (in some grammatical sense) of sentences
in which they occur; but nobody means to say that the
word "existence" itself is often the predicate of sentences
in which it occurs. And I think Mr. Kneale implies that,
similarly, the proposition which anyone would express, if
he asserted "Existence is a predicate," using "predicate"
in the logical sense, is again equivalent to a proposition,
not about the word "existence" itself, but about the word
"exists," and other finite parts of the verb "to exist." He
implies that "Existence is a predicate," with this use of
"predicate," is equivalent to the proposition that the word
"exists," and other finite parts of the verb, often do "*stand
for* a predicate in the logical sense." It would appear,
therefore, that one difference between the two different
meanings of "Existence is a predicate" is as follows: namely
that, if a person who says these words is using "predicate"
in the grammatical sense, he is *not* saying that the words,
"exists," etc., ever "*stand for* a predicate in the logical
sense;" whereas, if he is using "predicate" in the logical
sense, he is saying that they do (often, at least) "*stand for*
a predicate in the logical sense." What Mr. Kneale himself
means by "Existence is not a predicate" is apparently some

proposition which he would express by saying: "The words, 'exists,' etc., never stand for a predicate in the logical sense."

What I am not clear about is as to what is meant by saying of a particular word (or particular phrase) in a particular sentence that it "stands for a predicate in the logical sense;" nor, therefore, as to what is meant by saying of another particular word in another particular sentence that it does *not* "stand for a predicate in the logical sense." Mr. Kneale does, indeed, tell us that a "predicate in the logical sense" is the same as "an attribute;" but, though I think that the meaning of the word "attribute" is perhaps a little clearer than that of the phrase "predicate in the logical sense," it still seems to me far from clear: I do not clearly understand what he would mean by saying that "exists," etc., do not "stand for attributes." But, from examples which he gives, it is, I think, clear that he would say that in the sentence "This is red" the word "red," or the phrase "is red" (I am not clear which), does "stand for an attribute;" and also that in the sentence "Tame tigers growl," "growl" so stands, and in the sentence "Rajah growls," "growls" does. It is, therefore, presumably some difference between the way in which "exists," etc., are used in sentences in which they occur, and the way in which "is red" (or "red") and "growl" and "growls" are used in these sentences, that he wishes to express by saying that, whereas "exists," etc., do *not* "stand for attributes," these words in these sentences do. And if we can find what differences there are between the use of finite parts of the verb "to exist," and the use of "is red," "growl" and "growls," we may perhaps find what the difference is which he expresses in this way.

I

It will, I think, be best to begin with one particular use of "exist"—the one, namely, which Mr. Kneale illustrates by the example "Tame tigers exist." He clearly thinks that there is some very important difference between the way in which "exist" is used here, and the way in which "growl" is used in "Tame tigers growl;" and that it is a difference which does not hold, e.g. between the use of "scratch" in "Tame tigers scratch" and the use of "growl" in "Tame tigers growl." He would say that "scratch" and "growl" both "stand for attributes," whereas "exist" does not; and he would also say that "Tame tigers exist" is a proposition of a different *form* from "Tame tigers growl," whereas I think he would say that "Tame tigers growl" and "Tame tigers scratch" are *of the same form.* What difference between "Tame tigers exist" and "Tame tigers growl" can be the one he has in mind?

(1) That there is a difference between the way in which we use "exist" in the former sentence and "growl" in the latter, of a different kind from the difference between our usages of "scratch" and "growl" in the two sentences "Tame tigers scratch" and "Tame tigers growl," can, I think, be brought out in the following way.

The sentence "Tame tigers growl" seems to me to be ambiguous. So far as I can see, it might mean "All tame tigers growl," or it might mean merely "Most tame tigers growl," or it might mean merely "Some tame tigers growl." Each of these three sentences has a clear meaning, and the meaning of each is clearly different from that of either of the two others. Of each of them, however, it is true that the proposition which it expresses is one which cannot possibly be true, unless some tame tigers do growl. And hence I think we can say of "Tame tigers growl" that, whichever sense it is used in, it means something which cannot possibly be true unless some tame tigers do growl. Similarly I think it is clear that "Tame tigers exist" means something which cannot possibly be true unless some tame tigers do exist. But I do not think that there is any ambiguity in "Tame tigers exist" corresponding to that which I have pointed out in "Tame tigers growl." So far as I can see "Tame tigers exist" and "Some tame tigers exist" are merely two different ways of expressing exactly the same proposition. That is to say, it is not true that "Tame tigers exist" might mean "All tame tigers exist," or "Most tame tigers exist," instead of merely "Some tame tigers exist." It always means just "Some tame tigers exist," and nothing else whatever. I have said it is never used to mean "All tame tigers exist," or "Most tame tigers exist;" but I hope it will strike everyone that there is something queer about this proposition. It seems to imply that "All tame tigers exist" and "Most tame tigers exist" have a clear meaning, just as have "All tame tigers growl," and "Most tame tigers growl;" and that it is just an accident that we do not happen ever to use "Tame tigers exist" to express either of those two meanings instead of the meaning "Some tame tigers exist," whereas we do sometimes use "Tame tigers growl" to mean "All tame tigers growl" or "Most tame tigers growl," instead of merely "Some tame tigers growl." But is this in fact the case? Have "All tame tigers exist" and "Most tame tigers exist" any meaning at all? Certainly they have not a clear meaning, as have "All tame tigers growl" and "Most tame tigers growl." They are puzzling expressions, which certainly do not carry their meaning, if they have any, on the face of them. That this is so indicates, I think, that there is some important difference between the usage of "exist" with which we are concerned, and the usage of such words as "growl" or "scratch;" but it does not make clear just what the difference is.

I think this can be made clear by comparing the expressions "Some tame tigers don't growl" and "Some tame tigers don't exist." The former, whether true or false, has a perfectly clear meaning—a meaning just as clear as that of "Some tame tigers do growl;" and it is perfectly clear that both propositions might be true together. But with "Some tame tigers don't exist" the case is different. "Some tame tigers exist" has a perfectly clear meaning: it just means "There are some tame tigers." But the meaning of "Some tame tigers don't exist," if any, is certainly not equally clear. It is another queer and puzzling expression. Has it any meaning at all? and, if so, what meaning? If it has any, it would appear that it must mean the same as: "There are some tame tigers which don't exist." But has *this* any meaning? And if so, what? Is it possible that there should be any tame tigers which don't exist? I think the answer is that, if in the sentence "Some tame tigers don't exist," you are using "exist" with the same meaning as in "Some

tame tigers exist," then the former sentence as a whole has
no meaning at all—it is pure nonsense. A meaning can, of
course, be given to "Some tame tigers don't exist;" but this
can only be done if "exist" is used in a different way from
that in which it is used in "Some tame tigers exist." And,
if this is so, it will follow that "All tame tigers exist" and
"Most tame tigers exist," also have no meaning at all, if
you are using "exist" in the sense with which we are concerned. For "All tame tigers growl" is equivalent to the
conjunction "Some tame tigers growl, and there is no tame
tiger which does not growl;" and this has a meaning, because "There is at least one tame tiger which does not
growl" has one. If, therefore, "There is at least one tame
tiger which does not exist" has no meaning, it will follow
that "All tame tigers exist" also has none; because "There
is no tame tiger which does not exist" will have none, if
"There is a tame tiger which does not exist" has none.
Similarly "Most tame tigers growl" is equivalent to the
conjunction "Some tame tigers growl, and the number of
those (if any) which do not growl is smaller than that of
those which do"—a statement which has a meaning only
because "There are tame tigers which do not growl" has
one. If, therefore, "There are tame tigers which don't
exist" has no meaning, it will follow that "Most tame tigers
exist" will also have none. I think, therefore, we can say
that one important difference between the use of "growl"
in "Some tame tigers growl" and the use of "exist" in
"Some tame tigers exist," is that if in the former case we
insert "do not" before "growl," without changing the meaning of "growl," we get a sentence which is significant,
whereas if, in the latter, we insert "do not" before "exist"
without changing the meaning of "exist," we get a sentence
which has no meaning whatever; and I think we can also
say that this fact explains why, with the given meaning of
"growl," "All tame tigers growl" and "Most tame tigers
growl" are both significant, whereas, with the given meaning of "exist," "All tame tigers exist" and "Most tame
tigers exist" are utterly meaningless. And if by the statement that "growl," in this usage, "stands for an attribute,"
whereas "exist," in this usage, does not, part of what is

meant is that there is this difference between them, then I should agree that "exist," in this usage, does not "stand for an attribute."

But is it really true that if, in the sentence "Some tame tigers exist," we insert "do not" before "exist," without changing the meaning of "exist," we get a sentence which has no meaning whatever? I have admitted that a meaning *can* be given to "Some tame tigers do not exist;" and it may, perhaps, be contended by some people that the meaning which "exist" has in this sentence, where it is significant, *is* precisely the same as that which it has in "Some tame tigers exist." I cannot show the contrary as clearly as I should like to be able to do; but I will do my best.

The meaning which such an expression as "Some tame tigers do not exist" sometimes does have, is that which it has when it is used to mean the same as "Some tame tigers are imaginary" or "Some tame tigers are not real tigers." That "Some tame tigers are imaginary" may really express a proposition, whether true or false, cannot I think be denied. If, for instance, two different stories have been written, each of which is about a different imaginary tame tiger, it will follow that there are at least two imaginary tame tigers; and it cannot be denied that the sentence "Two different tame tigers occur in fiction" is significant, though I have not the least idea whether it is true or false. I know that at least one unicorn occurs in fiction, because one occurs in *Alice Through the Looking Glass;* and it follows that there is at least one imaginary unicorn, and therefore (in a sense) at least one unicorn which does not exist. Again, if it should happen that at the present moment two different people are each having an hallucination of a different tame tiger, it will follow that there are at the present moment two different imaginary tame tigers; and the statement that two such hallucinations are occurring now is certainly significant, though it may very likely be false. The sentence "There are some tame tigers which do not exist" is, therefore, certainly significant, if it means only that there are some imaginary tigers, in either of the two senses which I have tried to point out. But what it means is that either some real people have written stories about imaginary tigers, or are having or have recently had hallucinations of tame tigers, or, perhaps, are dreaming or have dreamed of particular tame tigers. If nothing of this sort has happened or is happening to anybody, then there are no imaginary tame tigers. But if "Some tame tigers do not exist" means all this, is it not clear that "exist" has not, in this sentence, the same comparatively simple meaning as it has in "Some tame tigers exist" or in "No tame tigers exist"? Is it not clear that "Some tame tigers do not exist," if it means all this, is not related to "Some tame tigers exist," in the same simple way in which "Some tame tigers do not growl" is related to "Some tame tigers growl"?

2. There is, I think, also another important difference between this use of "exist" and the use of "growl," which may be brought out as follows.

Mr. Russell has said "When we say 'some men are Greeks,' that means that the propositional function 'x is a man, and a Greek' is sometimes true;"[1] and has explained just previously that by "sometimes true" he means "true in at least one instance." With this explanation of what he means by "sometimes true," I do not think that his statement as to the meaning of "Some men are Greeks" is strictly correct; since I think that the use of the plural implies that "x is a man and a Greek" is true in *more* than one instance, that is to say, in at least two instances. Let us suppose that he would accept this correction and say that what "Some men are Greeks" means is not, strictly, that "x is a man and a Greek" is true in at least one instance, but that it is true in at least two. He has further implied[2] that to say of a propositional function that it is true in at least two instances is the same thing as to say that at least two "values" of it are true; and he has told us that the "values" of propositional functions are propositions.[3] With these explanations, his view would appear to be that what "Some men are Greeks" means is that at least two propositions, related to the propositional function

[1] *Introduction to Mathematical Philosophy* (1919), p. 159.
[2] *Ibid.*, p. 158.
[3] *Ibid.*, p. 156.

"x is a man and a Greek" in some way which he expresses
by saying that they are "values" of that function, are true.
Now I cannot imagine what sort of propositions would be
"values" of "x is a man and a Greek," except propositions
of the following sort. There are propositions which we
express by pointing at (or indicating in some other way),
an object which we are seeing (or perceiving in some
other way) and uttering the words "This is a so-and-so"
(or equivalent words in some other language). Let us
suppose that the kind of propositions which would be
"values" of "x is a man and a Greek" would be propositions
of this sort, where the words used were "This is a man and
a Greek." Mr. Russell's doctrine would then be that "Some
men are Greeks" means that at least two different true
propositions of this sort would be made: that there must
have been at least two different objects at which a man
might have pointed and said truly "This is a man and a
Greek." And, if this is his doctrine, it seems to me to be
true. Surely "Some men are Greeks" cannot possibly be
true, unless there are at least two different objects, in the
case of each of which a man might have seen it, pointed
at it, and said with truth "This is a man and a Greek"?

On this view "Some tame tigers growl" means that at
least two values of "x is a tame tiger and growls" are true;
and this means that there are at least two objects, in the
case of each of which a man might have seen it, pointed
at it, and said with truth "This is a tame tiger and growls."
Now in this sentence "This is a tame tiger and growls" it is
clear that, except for the difference consisting in the fact
that "growls" is in the singular and "growl" in the plural,
the word "growls" has the same meaning as has the word
"growl" in "Some tame tigers growl." We can say, then,
that one feature about our use of "growl" is that, if we
consider a "value" of the propositional function which is
such that "Some tame tigers growl" means that at least
two values of it are true, then the singular of "growl" can
be used, with the same meaning, in the expression of such
a value. And perhaps this may be part of what is meant by
saying that "growl" "stands for an attribute." It may perhaps be meant that to point at an object which you are

seeing, and utter the words "This object growls," is significant—that the words and gesture together do really express a proposition, true or false.

But now consider "Some tame tigers exist": is the same true of "exist" in this sentence? Mr. Russell says: "We say that 'men exist' or 'a man exists' if the propositional function 'x is human' is sometimes true."[4] And he goes on to protest that though the proposition "Socrates is a man" is "*equivalent*" to "Socrates is human," it "is not the very same proposition." For my part I doubt whether we ever do use "is human" in such a way that "Socrates is human" is equivalent to "Socrates is a man." I think Mr. Russell is using "is human" in a very special sense, in which nobody but he has ever used it, and that the only way of explaining how he is using it is to say that he is using it to mean precisely that which we ordinarily express by "is a human being." If this is so, and if we are allowed to distinguish, as I think we ought, between "men exist" and "a man exists," and to say that "men exist" means, *not* " 'x is a human being' is true in at least one instance," but " 'x is a human being' is true in at least two instances," then I think his doctrine is true; provided, again, that we are allowed to regard the sort of propositions which we express, e.g. by pointing at an object which we are seeing and saying the words "This is a human being," as being those which are values of "x is a human being." Surely "Human beings exist" can be true if, and only if, there are at least two objects, such that, if a man were to see and point to one of them and utter the words "This is a human being," he would be expressing a true proposition by what he did?

Now, if this is right, we see at once that the use of "growl" in "Some tame tigers growl" differs from that of "exist" in "Some tame tigers exist," in the respect that, while the first asserts that more than one value of "x is a tame tiger *and growls*" is true, the second asserts, *not* that more than one value of "x is a tame tiger *and exists*" is true, but merely that more than one value of "x is a tame tiger" is true. Owing to this view of his that "Some tame

[4] *Ibid.*, p. 171–72.

tigers exist" means the same as "Some values of the propositional function 'x is a tame tiger' are true," Mr. Russell has been led to say "Existence is essentially a property of a propositional function"[5] and "It is of propositional functions that you can assert or deny existence"[6] and that it is a fallacy to transfer "to the individual that satisfies a propositional function a predicate which only applies to a propositional function;"[7] so that, according to him, existence is, after all, in this usage, a "property" or "predicate," though not a property of individuals, but only of propositional functions! I think this is a mistake on his part. Even if it is true that "Some tame tigers exist" means the same as "Some values of 'x is a tame tiger' are true" it does not follow, I think, that we can say that "exist" means the same as "is sometimes true," and "some tame tigers" the same as "x is a tame tiger:" indeed, I think it is clear that we can not say this; for certainly " 'x is a tame tiger' exists" would not mean the same as "Some tame tigers exist." But what I think does follow from this interpretation of "Some tame tigers exist" is another thing which Mr. Russell himself holds, namely, that if a proposition which you express by pointing at something which you see and saying "This is a tame tiger," is a value of "x is a tame tiger," then if, pointing at the same thing, you were to say the words "This exists," and, if you were using "exists" merely as the singular of "exist" in the sense in which it is used in "Some tame tigers exist," what you did would not express a proposition at all, but would be absolutely meaningless. That is to say, there is between "Some tame tigers growl" and "Some tame tigers exist," not only the difference that, whereas the first asserts that some values of "x is a tame tiger *and growls*" are true, the second asserts only that some values of "x is a tame tiger" are true; there is also the further and more important difference that, why the second asserts only that some values of "x is a tame tiger" are true, is not because we happen to use "This is a tame tiger" to mean the same as "This is a tame tiger *and exists*,"

[5] *Monist*, April 1919, p. 195.
[6] *Ibid.*, p. 196.
[7] *Ibid.*, p. 197.

but because by pointing and saying "This *exists*" we should express *no proposition at all,* so long as we were using "exists" as the singular of the use of "exist" with which we are concerned, whereas by pointing and saying "This growls" we certainly should be expressing a proposition, even though we were using "growls" merely as the singular of "growl" with the meaning it has in "Some tame tigers growl." "This is a tame tiger, *and exists*" would be not tautologous, but meaningless.

This, I think, gives us a second true thing, which may perhaps be sometimes part of what is meant by saying that "exist," in this usage, "does not stand for an attribute."

II

So far I have been solely concerned with the use of "exist" in such sentences as "Some tame tigers exist," and have tried to point out two differences between its use here and the use of "growl" in "Some tame tigers growl," which may perhaps be part of what is meant by saying that "exist," in this usage, does not "stand for an attribute," whereas "growl" does. But I cannot help thinking that there are other significant uses of "exists;" and I want in particular, to try to point out two such, and to consider what, if anything, true can be meant by saying that in these usages also "exists" does not "stand for an attribute."

1. I have just said that to point at a thing which you see and say "This exists" seems to me to be meaningless, if "exists" is the singular of "exist" in the sense in which it is used in "Tame tigers exist;" but I cannot help thinking that in the case of anything to point at which and say "This is a tame tiger" is significant, it is also significant to point at it and say "This exists," *in some sense or other*. My reason for thinking this is that it seems to me that you can clearly say *with truth* of any such object "This *might* not have existed," "It is *logically possible* that this should not have existed;" and I do not see how it is possible that "This might not have existed" should be true, unless "This does in fact exist" is true, and therefore also significant. The statement "it is logically possible that this should not

have existed" seems to *mean* "The sentence 'This does not exist' is significant;" and if "This does not exist" is significant, "This does exist" must be significant too. Now I cannot help thinking that in every case in which I point at an object which I am perceiving and say significantly "This is a tame tiger," "This is a book," my proposition is in fact a proposition about some sense-datum, or some set of sense-data, which I am perceiving; and that part of what I am saying is that this sense-datum (or these sense-data) is "of" a physical object. That is to say, I am saying of some sense-datum that it is "of" a physical object in the sense in which it is true to say of an after-image which I see with my eyes shut that it is *not* "of" a physical object. And I think that part, at least, of what we mean by "This exists," where we are using "this" in the same way as when we point and say "This is a book," is "This sense-datum is of a physical object," which seems to me to be certainly significant. If "of" here stood for a relation we might say that "This is a book" was short for "The thing which this sense-datum is 'of' is a book," and therefore "This exists" short for "The thing which this sense-datum is 'of' exists;" in which case the use of "exists" in question would be that which in Principia Mathematica is symbolized by E!, and there would be the same sort of reason for saying that it does not "stand for an attribute" as in the case of the "exist" which occurs in "Some tame tigers exist." I do not believe, however, that "of" here does stand for a relation, nor therefore that "This" in "This is a book" can be said to be short for the sort of phrase which Russell has called "a definite description;" and, this being so, I am not at all clear as to what that is true could be meant by saying that "exists," in this usage, "does not stand for an attribute." The only suggestion I can make is this. It seems to me that "This exists" (in this usage) always forms part of what is asserted by "This is a book," "This is red," etc. etc., where "this" is used in the manner with which we are now concerned; and possibly part of what is meant by saying that "is a book," "is red," etc., "stand for attributes," is that *part but not the whole* of what is asserted by any "value" of "x is a book," "x is red," etc., is "This exists." In that case "exists" in "This exists" would not "stand for an attribute," solely because the whole of what it asserts, and not merely a part, is "This exists."

2. Another reason why "This exists," where "this" is used as it is in "This is a book" seems to me to be significant, is because it seems to me not only significant to say of a given sense-datum "This is of a physical object" or "This is not of a physical object," but also to say of the sense-datum itself "This exists." If this is so, we have to do with a new sense of "exists," since certainly no part of the meaning of such an assertion with regard to a sense-datum is that it, or any other sense-datum, is "of" a physical object. But my reason for holding that it is significant for me to say, for instance, of an after-image which I am seeing with my eyes shut, "This exists," is similar to that which I gave in the last case: namely that it seems to me that in the case of every sense-datum which anyone ever perceives, the person in question could always say with truth of the sense-datum in question "This might not have existed;" and I cannot see how this could be true, unless "This does in fact exist" is also true, and therefore significant. That "this exists" has any meaning in such cases, where, as Mr. Russell would say, we are using "this" as a "proper name" for something with which we are "acquainted," is, I know, disputed; my view that it has, involves, I am bound to admit, the curious consequence that "this exists," when used in this way, is always true, and "this does not exist" always false; and I have little to say in its favour except that it seems to me so plainly true that, in the case of every sense-datum I have, it is logically possible that the sense-datum in question should not have existed —that there should simply have been no such thing. If, for instance, I am seeing a bright after-image with my eyes shut, it seems to me quite plainly conceivable that I should have had instead, at that moment, a uniform black field, such as I often have with my eyes shut; and, if I had had such a field, then that particular bright after-image simply would not have existed.

But, supposing "This exists," in this usage, has a meaning, why should we not say that "exists" here "stands for an attribute"? I can suggest no reason why we should not, except the same which I suggested in the last case.

9. WILLIAM P. ALSTON (1921–   )

[*William P. Alston, professor of philosophy at the University of Michigan, has written extensively on the philosophy of language and the philosophy of logic. Here he expresses dissatisfaction with the traditional attempts to refute the ontological argument. He does not, however, believe the argument is sound, and provides what he considers a new refutation of it.*]

THE ONTOLOGICAL ARGUMENT REVISITED*

The ontological argument has often been criticized on the grounds that it mistakenly supposes "exists" to be a predicate. I am going to argue (1) that the way in which this criticism is usually presented is faulty, (2) that these faults result from overlooking certain basic features of the concept of existence, and (3) that when these features are fully taken into account, new and sounder reasons can be given for denying that "exists" is a predicate and for rejecting the ontological argument. In the first section I shall present the traditional kind of criticism in what I take to be its strongest form; in the second, I shall try to show that it does not hold up; in the third I shall attempt to enrich it so as to avoid those defects.[1]

* From *The Philosophical Review*, Vol. LXIX (1960). Reprinted by permission of the author and the Editorial Board of *The Philosophical Review*.

[1] It may be helpful to relate this essay to Professor Norman Malcolm's very interesting article, "Anselm's Ontological Arguments," which recently appeared in the *Review* (LXIX, 1960, 41–62) [this volume, p. 136]. There Malcolm distinguishes two

I

Undoubtedly the ontological argument does depend on using "exists" as a predicate.

> . . . each time I happen to think of a first and sovereign being, and to draw, so to speak, the idea of him from the storehouse of the mind, I am necessitated to *attribute* to him all kinds of perfections, though I may not then enumerate them all, nor think of each of them in particular. And this necessity is sufficient, as soon as I discover that *existence is a perfection,* to cause me to infer the existence of this first and sovereign being: just as it is not necessary that I should ever imagine any triangle, but whenever I am desirous of considering a rectilineal figure composed of only three angles, it is absolutely necessary to *attribute* those *properties* to it from which it is correctly inferred that its three angles are not greater than two right angles . . .[2]

It is clear that Descartes is assuming a logical parallel between "A triangle has angles equal to two right angles" and "A perfect being exists."[3] There is no conceivable alternative to the former, because having its angles equal to two right angles is part of what we mean by a triangle, or at least follows from part of what we mean by a triangle.

different arguments in Anselm's *Proslogion.* My treatment of Anselm is restricted to what Malcolm calls the first argument, and is concerned with the sort of considerations which are commonly used in rejecting it. About what Malcolm calls the second argument, I have nothing to say in this essay. My opinion is that the second argument is ultimately dependent on the first, but that is a long story.

[2] R. Descartes, *Meditation V,* trans. J. Veitch (La Salle, Illinois, 1937), pp. 79–80. Italics mine.

[3] Of course it may be doubted that the former is logically necessary, or at least that "the predicate is contained in the subject." But since we are not at present concerned with mathematics, we can ignore this. It is enough that Descartes treats this statement as if the predicate were contained in the subject.

Likewise there is no conceivable alternative to predicating "exists" of a perfect being, since existing is part of what we mean by a perfect being (existence is a perfection). In both cases we simply attribute to the entity one of the properties which serve as a necessary condition of its being the thing it is. Without this logical parallel the principle from which Descartes starts—". . . because I can draw from my thought the idea of an object, it follows that all I clearly and distinctly apprehend to pertain to this object, does in truth belong to it"[4]—would have no application to the existence of God.

What reasons are there to deny that "exists" is a predicate? Where the support for this denial goes beyond pious asseveration, which is less often than one would like to think, it usually takes the form of pointing out logical differences between admitted subject-predicate statements and statements which differ from these only in the substitution of "exists" for the predicate.[5] But it is never shown that these differences are such as to prevent "exists" from being a predicate, rather than making it a very special sort of predicate, as a stubborn Cartesian might insist. After all, there are very great logical differences between admitted subject-predicate statements, too. To remedy this deficiency, it is necessary to exhibit the nature of predication. Until we have made explicit what it is to predicate, we are not likely to determine conclusively whether or not a given term is capable of being predicated. Now without going beyond the orbit of the traditional critique, I want to try to give it a stronger and more fundamental formulation than it usually receives. Only when the traditional criticism is stated in the strongest possible form will its basic defects be seen clearly.

I am incapable of giving, nor is it necessary for my purpose to give, an exhaustive analysis of predication. It will

[4] *Ibid.*, p. 77.
[5] For a good example of this, see G. E. Moore, "Is Existence a Predicate?," *Proceedings of the Aristotelian Society*, supp. vol. XV (1936). Reprinted in A. Flew (ed.), *Logic and Language* (Second Series; Oxford, 1953).

suffice to bring out one of its essential features. Before we can attach any predicate to anything ("round," "heavy," "in my pocket," "belongs to Jones," "difficult to understand"), we must presuppose that it exists. If we were not making that assumption we could not even raise the question whether a given predicate attaches to it. To predicate sweetness of the pie in the oven without presupposing that there is a pie in the oven would be as self-defeating as asking you to take the pie out of the oven, or asking you whether the pie in the oven is done, without that supposition. But we must put this point carefully. I can *deceitfully* say that the pie in the oven is sweet, knowing all along that there is no pie in the oven, just as I can deceitfully ask you to take it out, knowing there is none. Still, there is an important sense in which I am, even here, presupposing that there is a pie in the oven. This sense can be brought out as follows: one (logically) could not openly admit that *a* does not exist (or doubt, wonder, or express ignorance about whether *a* exists) and still predicate *P* of *a*. This would be logically impossible simply because in the face of this admission we would not (could not) interpret what the speaker says as predicating *P* of *a*. "There is no pie in the oven, and the pie in the oven is sweet" cannot be used to make a predication, though it might be used to propound a riddle, be ironical, or test one's voice.

On this basis it is easy to show that "exists" cannot be a predicate. If the existence of the subject must be presupposed before we can set about attaching (withholding, wondering whether to attach) any predicate to (from) it, we will always be too late either to apply or to withhold a predicate of existence. The application of such a predicate would simply repeat the preliminary conditions for any predication. (Compare "I am speaking," "You are being spoken to.") And the denial of such a predicate would contradict the essential conditions of any predication. (Compare "I am not speaking," "You are not being spoken to.") In other words, on the predicative interpretation, any positive existential statement, for example, "A perfect tennis player exists," would be trivial. Since I must already have settled (or pretend to have settled) the existence of a perfect tennis player before I can say anything about him, going on to say that he exists would just be going over something which had already been completed behind the scenes. But obviously such an assertion is not trivial; it constitutes a substantive claim, whereas any negative existential ("A perfect tennis player does not exist") on the predicative interpretation would be self-defeating. If I first presuppose that a perfect tennis player exists and then go ahead to deny existence, I am taking away with one hand what was offered with the other. I am destroying an essential condition of what I set out to say. And equally obviously, not all negative existentials are self-defeating. We do sometimes succeed in denying the existence of something.[6]

The application of all this to the ontological argument is obvious. Descartes can get from the principle "Perfection implies existence" or "Existence is a perfection" to the conclusion he wants, "A perfect being exists," only by using that principle to show that existence must be predicated of a perfect being. But we can predicate, or refuse to predicate, anything of a perfect being, only if we purport to have already settled that there is a perfect being. However true it may be that being unmarried is contained in the notion of bachelorhood, I cannot conclude that it is necessarily true that the bachelor next door is unmarried, unless I have been assured that there is a bachelor next door.

II

It is my contention that this line of criticism is vitiated by the neglect of important distinctions. The heart of the argument, let us remember, was the claim that any attempted predication of existence where positive would be

---

[6] This argument has been presented by several recent writers, but without clearly exhibiting its dependence on the nature of predication. See C. D. Broad, *Religion, Philosophy, and Psychical Research* (London, 1953), pp. 182–83; John Wisdom, *Interpretation and Analysis* (London, 1931), p. 62; A. J. Ayer, *Language, Truth, and Logic* (2nd ed.; London, 1947), p. 43.

trivial, and where negative would be self-defeating. I now wish to show that this is not always so. But first a note on procedure. It should be clear from the above that I side with Strawson against Russell in denying that "The *P* is *Q*" can be accurately translated by "There is one and only one *x* which is *P*, and anything which is *P* is *Q*"; the reason being that the former presupposes the first conjunct of the latter rather than explicitly asserts it. Nevertheless the triviality of (1A) "The *P* exists" can be most clearly exhibited by making the presupposition explicit and showing the redundancy of (2A) "There is one and only one *P* and it exists." And it would be true to say that the triviality of (1A) rests on the redundancy of (2A). In the same way the self-defeating character of (1B) "The *P* does not exist" could be said to rest on the contradictoriness of (2B) "There is one and only one *P*, and it does not exist." Since these more explicit models reveal more sharply the logical features in which we are interested, it will be more convenient, and perfectly harmless, to work with them, even if they are not strict synonyms of the ones in which we are ultimately interested.

A. My contention is that 2A-form statements are not always redundant, and that 2B-form statements are not always self-contradictory. To an ear dulled by the habitual blurring of distinctions in philosophical discourse, this may seem outrageous. But in fact plainly substantive statements of this form occur fairly often.

(A) There are centaurs in Greek mythology, but no such creatures exist.

(B) In many old legends there is a British king named Arthur who leads the British against the Saxons, and, according to some scholars, he really existed.

Lest it should be supposed that such statements depend on a difference in meaning between "there is" and "exists," consider other examples which do not exhibit this terminological shift.

(C) That ghost exists only in your imagination. (It does not really exist.)

(D) Perfectly unselfish people exist only in literature.
(No such people really exist.)[7]

In citing these sentences as counter-instances, I am so
construing them that the phrases "in Greek mythology,"
"in literature," "in your imagination," and so forth, modify
"there is" and "exists," thereby specifying what sort of
existence is being asserted. On this interpretation, in uttering one of these sentences, one would be asserting that
something has one mode of existence, and then denying
that the same thing has another mode of existence. But
this interpretation may be questioned. Why not read (A)
like "There are kangaroos in Australia, but kangaroos do
not exist in South America." No one would claim the latter
to be of the 2B form. The prepositional phrases plainly
belong with the specification of what is said to exist. It is
kangaroos in Australia which we are saying there are,
kangaroos in South America which we are saying there
are not. Kangaroos *überhaupt* are not in the picture at all.
If we adopt this sort of interpretation for our examples,
they do no damage to the standard argument. Once we
fully specify what is claimed to exist in each clause, it is
plain that we are not really asserting and denying existence
of the same thing.

But this alternative interpretation will not hold water.
On this interpretation there is one and only one mode of
existence, which things can be said to have in various
places—Australia, Tahiti, or the Milky Way. But once we
stretch the notion of place to include fiction, mythology,
imagination, and the real world, it becomes very unclear

---

[7] In treating these sentences as of the same form as 2A and
2B, I am taking "there is" and "exists" to be roughly synonymous, wherever grammar allows the use of either. And the "one
and only one" qualifier is not important for the present problem.
Hence all the following sorts of statements can be counted as of
the same form as 2B (and parallels could easily be constructed
for 2A):

There are *P*'s . . . . , but they do not exist . . . . . .
P's exist . . . . , but they do not exist . . . .
A *P* exists. . . . . , but it does not exist . . . .
There is an *x* named "*P*" . . . . , but it does not exist . . . .
That *P* exists . . . . , but it does not exist . . . .

what could be meant by the existence which could in-differently be exercised in these locales. We can under-stand one sort of existence being possessed either in Aus-tralia or Greenland, but that is because we are holding it constant to, say, real as opposed to fictional existence. Vary that, too, and with what are we left? I can say "There (really) is a key to this box" without saying where the key is, and I have told you something, though perhaps you would like to have fuller information. But if I say "Sea serpents exist," and leave it open whether I mean in my-thology, in literature, in reality, or in my imagination, what have I told you? Have I excluded anything? Can I con-ceive of anything which would not exist in at least one of these "places"? It seems that I must, implicitly or ex-plicitly, add one of these qualifications in order to get any assertion at all. This means that "in literature," "in reality," and so forth, are not independent of "exists" in the way "in my pocket" and "in Labrador" are. (This is the justi-fication for denying that existence is a genus. To assign something to a genus without giving its species is to give real, though relatively abstract, information. The generic term stands on its own feet predicatively, whereas, as we have just seen, we must have in mind some specific mode of existence in order to get an assertion.) The supposition that "There are centaurs in Greek mythology, but they do not exist in reality" is properly analyzed as "($\exists x$) (x is a centaur in Greek mythology) and $\sim$ ($\exists x$) (x is a centaur in reality)," breaks down through inability to give any interpretation to "$\exists$" which is common to both these occurrences.

Hence the standard argument against treating "exists" as a predicate collapses. If I can say, without redundancy, "There is in many old legends a British King named Arthur who fought against the Saxons, and the evidence is that he really existed," it would seem that I can just as well set up a subject on the presupposition of the first conjunct, and then, without triviality, predicate real existence of this subject. And if I can, without contradiction, say "There are centaurs in Greek mythology, but centaurs do not really exist," it would seem that I can presuppose the first conjunct in setting up legendary centaurs as subjects of predication, and then, without self-stultification, deny that the predicate of real existence attaches to these subjects. The way is then open to regarding "King Arthur really existed" and "Centaurs do not really exist" as subject-predicate statements. We can use one mode of existence to set up the subject, and another mode of existence as the predicate. At least, once we recognize diverse modes of existence, the standard arguments are powerless to prevent this.

And this means that the ontological argument has not finally been disposed of. Granted different modes of existence, we can restate the argument in a form which is not open to the standard objections. We can get our subject of predication by presupposing the existence of a perfect being in some nonreal mode, where the existence is obvious. Then we can argue that an analysis of this being shows that it possesses the characteristic of real existence.

It is interesting that St. Anselm's version of the ontological argument (in his *Proslogium*) is explicitly in this form. The difference between Anselm and Descartes in this regard has been too little remarked. Instead of saying, with Descartes, that existence is contained in the idea of a perfect being, Anselm speaks of a being than which nothing greater can be conceived, which he initially supposes to have a certain kind of existence—existence in the understanding. He takes considerable pains to justify this presupposition.

> . . . the fool hath said in his heart, there is no God (Psalm xiv. 1). But, at any rate, this very fool, when he hears of this being of which I speak—a being than which nothing greater can be conceived—understands what he hears, and what he understands is in his understanding; . . . . Hence even the fool is convinced that something exists in the understanding, at least, than which nothing greater can be conceived. For, when he hears of this, he understands it. And whatever is understood, exists in the understanding.

He can then raise the question of what can (or must) be
attributed to this being; the argument is, of course, that
real existence must, on pain of contradiction, be attributed
to it.

> And assuredly that, than which nothing greater can
> be conceived, cannot exist in the understanding alone.
> For, suppose it exists in the understanding alone: then
> it can be conceived to exist in reality; which is greater.
>
> Therefore, if that, than which nothing greater can
> be conceived, exists in the understanding alone, the
> very being, than which nothing greater can be con-
> ceived, is one, than which a greater can be conceived.
> But obviously this is impossible.[8]

In this form the argument has recognized the principle
that all predication presupposes the existence of a subject,
and so is not subject to any attack based on this principle.

And yet we know something must be wrong. Else the
perfect island, et al., return to haunt (or enchant) us.

B. Before giving my diagnosis I must take notice of a
protest which, if heeded, would obviate the need for one.
It may take many forms: "Being in literature is not existing in any sense." " 'Existing in legend' is just a way of
talking about what people say when they repeat legends."
"Since 'existing in the understanding' is just a misleading
reformulation of 'have an idea of,' Anselm is not really
different from Descartes."

So far as these protests simply amount to an *exclusion*
of such phrases as "exists in your imagination" (perhaps on
the grounds that only real existence is *real* existence), they
can be safely ignored. But a more serious thesis may be
concealed therein. It may be claimed that all other types
of existence can be reduced to real existence, that we
could say everything we ever want to say without employing such phrases. For example, instead of saying "There
are centaurs in Greek mythology," we could do the same

[8] St. Anselm, *Proslogium,* trans. by S. N. Deane (Chicago,
1939), ch. II.

job by saying "In the recitation of their myths the ancient Greeks used a word or phrase synonymous with 'centaur.'" Similarly, "There were three flying saucers in my dream" can be replaced by "I dreamed about three flying saucers," or "In my dream it was as if I were seeing three flying saucers"; and "That ghost exists only in your imagination" becomes "You are just imagining a ghost." Similarly, "The perfect being exists in the understanding" will, when fumigated, become "We can form a concept of a perfect being," which may in turn be transformed into "We can learn how to use the phrase 'perfect being.'" In these replacements the only sort of existence which is asserted or presupposed is real existence.

Doubts could be expressed as to the feasibility of such a general reduction. For example, in "You are just imagining a ghost," is "a ghost" a referring phrase? And if it is, are we presupposing a nonreal mode of existence for a ghost? But even granted that it could be carried through, what bearing would it have on our present problem? Well, in a language which is stripped down in this way, the standard argument against the possibility of predicating existence would hold good, and for that reason the ontological argument could not be given a valid formulation in such a language. But that falls short of showing that in language as we have it the argument collapses. I am sure Anselm would be willing to settle for the validity of his argument in ordinary medieval Latin. But, says the reconstructionist, the languages are different only in form, not in content. This follows from the premise that everything sayable in the one is equally sayable in the other. Hence the fact that existence cannot be a predicate in the revised language shows that, despite appearances, it cannot be a predicate in ordinary language either. But there are two difficulties with this. (1) How do we know which way to read the equivalence? What if Anselm said, "The fact that existence can be used as a predicate in ordinary language shows that, despite appearances, it can be so used in the revised language"? (2) We have not explored all the complications involved in the claim that in each of the above pairs the one sentence can be used to say just what is said by the other. Once Anselm saw that in the second language he could not say that the most perfect being necessarily exists, he would have second thoughts about his admission that the two are equally rich. More generally, whenever any translation gets rid of some supposed metaphysical presupposition or implication, but otherwise preserves the meaning of the original, those who want to preserve this metaphysical concomitant, once they see what is going on, will refuse to admit the accuracy of the translation. But it is just such folk for whom the translation is designed. (Compare translating "Courage is a virtue" into "Anyone who is courageous is virtuous," in order to get rid of universals; or "The fact that he took bribes is well known" into "Many people knew that he took bribes," in order to get rid of facts.)

These are special cases of ills which are endemic to reductionism. The apparent use of "exists" as a predicate, and its most famous offspring, the ontological argument, arose in language as we actually have it. It is in the course of using that language that we have fallen under the spell of this argument. The spell will not be broken by showing that the incantations could not be intoned in another language, however akin it may be in other respects. So long as we are under the spell, the fact that it gives no place to those incantations shows that it is not close enough. What we must do is to discover what, if anything, there is in language as we use it that prevents the use of "exists" as a predicate (and spikes the ontological argument). If that cannot be done, then the proposed revision is invalid as well as inept. If using "exists" as a predicate is possible in ordinary language, then any language in which this is not possible is not equivalent.[9]

[9] If it could be shown that the rules of ordinary language are inconsistent on this point, that would alter the situation. In that case these rules would have to be altered in some way. But no one has shown that a reduction of fictional to real existence is needed to avoid inconsistency, or even unintelligibility. No one has shown that employing "exists" as we ordinarily do leads us into contradictions. The virtues which could be plausibly claimed for the reduction would be, rather, economy and the avoidance of possible confusions.

III

What is wrong with predicating real existence of a perfect being which exists in the understanding? There are many predications which are plainly all right here. We can say of this being that it is infinite, wise, just, merciful, all-knowing, and so forth. But when we add "and really exists," something jars us; we are seized with logical vertigo. This, we want to say, is different. But can this feeling be justified? What is so different about it? Well, in all the other cases, we remained within the sphere of ideas or concepts, but when real existence is asserted we step outside that sphere, and this cannot be done solely from an examination of its contents. We must look outside and see what is there. Dissection of what is in the understanding can never tell us what is in the real world, any more than analysis of my dreams will ever tell me which of their contents, if any, faithfully represent real objects (at least not without some dream theory which is itself partly based on evidence concerning real things), or any more than any literary analysis of the character of Achilles in the *Iliad* can determine whether this is a historical figure. To do this would mean lifting ourselves by our bootstraps, or unlocking a door by staring at the lock.

But, comes the inevitable rejoinder, this case is different. In general it is true that one cannot show that *x* really exists simply by analyzing its existence in the understanding. But here is the one case where this is possible. Here the nature of the being in the understanding is of such ontological richness as to burst its bonds; its inherent expansive power impels it across the boundary into real existence.

These metaphors get us nowhere. We cannot cross the border without a passport which has been approved on the other side, but a rocket can, with luck, burst into outer space on the strength of energy developed within the earth's atmosphere. And so it goes. Which of these metaphors is the more illuminating? Is deciding whether an envisaged being really exists more like applying for a passport or rocketing into space? Evidently we need a more literal characterization of the situation. Here is such a characterization.

A. Earlier we saw that an existential statement has the function of setting up a subject for predication. Now that we have recognized different modes of existence we can add a further stipulation: the kind of existence which is being stated will place limits on the sorts of predication that can be made with respect to that subject, that is, on the logical status of statements which can be made about it. A few examples should make this clear.

1. As I come into the house, I hear my wife who, unbeknownst to me, is reading a story to some children, say, "The cookies in the pantry are delicious." Being hungry, I go to the pantry, but am disappointed to find the cookies there stale and tasteless, whereupon I upbraid my wife for deception.

2. In a discussion of Dostoevski's *The Brothers Karamazov* in which undue emphasis was being given to Dmitri and Alyosha, someone might say, "After all, old man Karamazov had three sons." An unlettered youth who had just come into the group might ask, "Are any of them still living?"

3. A physics student tells me that the electrons of which my desk is composed are moving around with great speed. When I ask him how powerful a microscope would be needed to see them, he replies that they cannot be seen through any existing microscope, nor would he expect to see them through any microscope, no matter how powerful, whereupon I accuse him of talking nonsense.

In these cases a subject-predicate statement was misunderstood because of a misapprehension as to the kind of existence being presupposed. Under this misapprehension the hearers took the statements to have a kind of logical status they lacked. In particular, the statements were misinterpreted as to their implications, theoretical or practical. The statements were mistakenly supposed to have the following implications:

1. A hungry man who wants good cookies would be well advised to go into the pantry.
2. Either the sons of Karamazov are still living, or they have died since the time under discussion.
3. If one could achieve sufficient power of magnification, he could see the ultimate particles of which this desk is composed.

A mistake was also made concerning the considerations and procedures relevant to supporting or attacking the statements:

1. Examination of the contents of the pantry.
2. Questioning of elderly citizens in the neighborhood or friends of the family. Consultation of official records.
3. Scanning the desk through the highest-power microscope available.

Generalizing from these cases, we can say that the kind of considerations which are relevantly adduced in defending or attacking a subject-predicate statement, and the sorts of implications which can be drawn from it, are a function (in part) of the kind of existence presupposed. Presuppose that there were three flying saucers in my dream, and nothing tells for or against any statement about these three objects except my (sincere) report. But presuppose that there really were three flying saucers over the Grand Canyon yesterday, and now the testimony of others, consideration of laws of aerodynamics, and so forth, become relevant to the evaluation of statements about them. Presuppose that there was a King of the Round Table in legend, and all sorts of statements about him can be conclusively established by an examination of documents like *Morte d'Arthur*, without looking into their historical accuracy. But presuppose that there was a real historical king who had such a court, and much more is needed. Whether or not the statement "That ghost is in the house again" implies that abnormal phenomena are to be expected in the house in the immediate future depends on whether the assumption on which that statement rests is that a certain ghost exists in your imagination, or that a certain ghost really exists. "The men from Mars are approaching Plainfield, New Jersey" implies that Plainfield, New Jersey is in imminent danger only if real existence has been presupposed for men from Mars.

Note that in general it is the logical status of the predication which is delimited, not the possible predicates themselves. In general anything that can be said of a real man can be said of a legendary, fictional, or imaginary man. It is what gets said in applying any predicate which will differ in the way specified above.

Thus an existential statement determines a logical framework within which predications can be made of what has been said to exist. It can be construed as a license to make certain sorts of subject-predicate statements, and not others. In fact we might take the determination of such logical frameworks as a principle of differentiation for modes of existence. If the same logical status is conferred, then there is only one mode of existence in question. It is on this kind of ground that we might refuse to distinguish between existing in the understanding and existing in the mind, or between the mode of existence involved in existing in Australia and existing in South America, while insisting on a distinction between either of the first pair and either of the second.

One more step is needed before we can return, sufficiently girded, to the ontological argument. An existential statement has the same sorts of implications as the subject-predicate statements it licenses and to that extent falls within the logical framework it determines. This principle might be defended by saying that a licensing bureau cannot authorize anyone to do anything it does not have the authority to do, but this would be riding the metaphor too hard, or else regressing to the scholastic principle "The cause must contain at least as much perfection as the effect." A more sober defense would run like this. It seems that an existential statement not only permits a certain kind of subject-predicate statement but also guarantees that there will be true statements of that kind. To say that there really are sea serpents is to imply that there are true statements of the form "Sea serpents are . . ." which have the logical status of statements about physical objects. To say that there are P's is to imply that something can be truly said about them. This entailment can be brought out by considering the logical oddity of the following dialogue.

A. There are a lot of bones six feet under my back yard.

B. Well, what about them?

A. Nothing. They are just there, that's all.

B. You mean you haven't looked at any of them yet?

A. No. It's not that I haven't found out anything about them yet. There is nothing to find out, except that they are there.

Why is this? Why do we refuse to admit the possibility that there are things about which nothing can be truly (synthetically) predicated? Perhaps it is because a referring expression is used to direct attention to something which goes beyond the characteristics connoted by the expression. If nothing could be said of the bones under my back yard other than that they are bones under my back yard, there would be no distinctive use for a referring expression here or for the subject-predicate form within which it gets its use. There would be no point in distinguishing between "the bones under my back yard" and "bone under my back yard." The point in talking about *things which are* bones under my back yard is that each of those things possesses characteristics other than those connoted by the descriptive phrase used to refer to it. The very concept of a thing (and of its linguistic correlates, the referring expression and the subject-predicate sentence) requires such an overplus.

B. Now we can return to the ontological argument in its Anselmian form. Anselm escapes the standard criticism by presupposing existence in the understanding so as to get a subject of which he can show real existence to be necessarily predicated. But an equally unhappy fate awaits him. The statement which he is claiming to be necessarily true is a statement about a being in the understanding, and as such exhibits the logical features of statements based on a presupposition of mental existence. Among these features are: (1) It can be conclusively tested, if at all, by reflection. The person in whose understanding a certain being exists has only to reflect, to ask himself what he means by a certain term, in order to determine whether or not any statement about that being is true. A simple and instantaneous self-question is all that is needed to enable me to state with complete assurance that the girl of my dreams has eyes of blue. Nothing could possibly shake that assurance. (2) Existence in the understanding shares with other nonreal modes of existence the following features. For each existent in some nonreal mode, we can specify two sorts of real existents. First, there is some real existent of a given sort, which is always of the same sort for a given nonreal mode, the existence of which is entailed by the nonreal existence of the thing in question. Whenever something exists in my dreams, there must be a real conscious dream state; whenever something exists in legend or myth, there are real activities of repeating, hearing, thinking about the legends and myths in question; whenever something exists in my understanding, there are real thoughts, ideas, images, and so forth, in my mind which would ordinarily be said to be about this thing, perhaps real dispositions to behave in certain ways toward things of this kind, and so forth. It is this entailment which lends plausibility to the project of reducing all other modes of existence to real existence. Let us call such a real existent the *real correlate* of a nonreal existent. Second, we can specify something which really exists and has all the characteristics (excluding existence, if that exclusion is necessary) of the nonreal existent. Let us call this the *real archetype* of the nonreal existent. Thus the real archetype of a mountain in my dream would be a real mountain of the same size, shape, and so forth; the real archetype of Ivanhoe would be a Saxon nobleman of the twelfth century who did (some of) the things with which this character in Scott's novel was credited.

Now it seems to be a defining feature of all nonreal modes of existence that any statement about something which exists in such a mode will have no implications with respect to real things, except for its real correlate and any implications that might have. In particular it has no implications concerning the real archetype. This latter is an essential feature of the concept of different modes of existence. If the existence of something in one mode should imply its existence in another mode, the distinction between these two modes would crumble. To say that (the legendary) King Arthur won twelve battles implies nothing about the political or military fortunes of the past, or about historical records of the present and future, except that certain unspecified individuals have said and heard such things in legend-reciting contexts. To say that the mountains in my dream had very sharp peaks has no geographical implications; it is of significance not to the map-maker but to the psychoanalyst. Likewise any statement which attaches a predicate to something which exists in my understanding can have no implications for the real world except for the fact that I have, or have had, certain thoughts.

This means that if "The being than which nothing greater can be conceived exists in reality" is to be interpreted as the attribution of a predicate to a being in the understanding, it can have no implications with respect to the real world other than the fact that Anselm, or whoever else forms this concept, had a certain idea in his mind. But it is plain that as this sentence would ordinarily be understood, it implies much more than this about the real world. In accordance with the principle enunciated above, this existential statement implies that there are some true statements about a really existing perfect being, having the sorts of implications that such statements typically have; and in addition it specifically implies the truth of any statement of the form "The perfect being is P," where P is analytically contained in perfection, together with whatever implications such statements as these have. And it is equally plain that Anselm understands it, and purports to have established it, in this sense. The ensuing sections of the *Proslogium* make it plain that he supposed his thesis to entail the following propositions (by way of the fact that perfection analytically entails omnipotence and perfect goodness): (1) everything in the world is arranged for the best; (2) the righteous will ultimately be rewarded and the guilty will be punished, at least those who are not pardoned by divine mercy; (3) the world causally depends for its existence on a perfect spiritual being; (4) every man is under an obligation to worship and seek a real contact with this being. Obviously none of this follows from the fact that Anselm or anyone else has certain thoughts.

Thus Anselm, though more subtle than Descartes, is finally brought to the same pass. "The perfect being exists in reality" can only be claimed to be necessarily true, at least on the grounds adduced by Anselm, provided we construe "exists in reality" as a predicate of the perfect being, the existence of which in the understanding has been presupposed. But this gives us a statement the logical status of which sharply distinguishes it from an ordinary statement of real existence and prevents it from having the sort of religious significance for the sake of which the conclusion was sought. If, per contra, we make a statement of real existence in the ordinary sense, which has the sort of implications we want, this prevents it from being construed as the attribution of a property to a being which exists in the understanding, and neither Anselm nor anyone else has given any reasons for considering the statement to be necessary.

At this point we might get the old refrain, "But this case is different. It is generally true that statements about nonreal existents can have no implications for reality outside their real correlates. But this principle gained its plausibility from a survey of cases which omitted the one in hand. Here is the one case to which they do not apply. In this one case a statement about a mental being has implications for the real world outside our ideas and thoughts, for this case is unique in that the predicate involved is real existence. And this claim cannot be overthrown by the use of principles built on other cases, from which this one differs in crucial respects."

But it is too late in the day for this maneuver. The claim

to be examining this case in itself will not hold up. Such an examination, however narrowly concentrated, must make use of general terms like "predicate," "exists in reality," and the like, and its (apparent) force depends on (apparently) using these terms in their ordinary senses. If Anselm did not suppose "The perfect being exists in reality" to be a predication in the ordinary sense of "predication," his argument that this statement is necessary could never get off the ground. If he were not using "exists in the understanding" in its customary sense, his existential presupposition would have no force; if he were not using "exists in reality" in its ordinary sense, his conclusion would not have the religious relevance for the sake of which it was sought. It is essential for his argument that this case *not* be different in the sense given these terms. But my argument depended solely on an elucidation of the ordinary senses of these terms. It is impossible that there should be exceptions to the principles I have been invoking, so long as we are using "predicate," "really exists," and so forth, in the usual way. Thus Anselm is barred from claiming idiosyncrasy for his case in any way which would confer exemption from these principles.

C. It might look as if this revised critique of the ontological argument has been developed without relying on the denial that "exists" is a predicate; indeed, without having refurbished that denial after it had collapsed in the face of a plurality of modes of existence. But this would be a superficial view. The above considerations have only to be generalized to provide a revised proof that "exists" is not a predicate.

The standard argument was seen to be faulty in failing to rule out the possibility that statements of real existence, for example, could be construed as attributions of real existence to a subject which had been assumed to exist in some other mode. But now a closer look at the distinctions between the various modes of existence has shown them to be unfitted for this role. We have seen that no statement which attributes something to a nonreal being can have the logical status (implications, and so forth) of a statement of real existence. Hence this attempt to interpret real existence as a predicate collapses. This argument can then be further generalized to show that no mode of existence can be construed as an attribute. For the mode of existence presupposed by the subject term (which has to be different from the mode of existence predicated, or the traditional argument comes back into force) will give the statement a logical status which will inevitably fail to coincide with the status it must have if it is to be a statement of existence of the sort embodied in the (supposed) predicate. Thus if we try to construe "King Arthur exists in legend" as the attribution of legendary existence to a subject presupposed to exist in the imagination, we run into the difficulty that no statement about what exists in the imagination can have the sort of implications about what goes on in legend-narrating activities that a statement of legendary existence must have. And if we try to construe "There were two of the Karamazov brothers in my dream" as attributing dream-existence to two men who are presupposed as having fictional existence, we run afoul of the fact that my statement has implications as to what was going on in my consciousness during the night which no statement about fictional characters can have.

I am not saying, of course, that we cannot make a transition from one mode of existence to another. We can consider a mythological figure, a character in fiction, a scene in a dream, or a theoretically envisaged entity like a cosmic designer or a solar vortex, and ask whether it also really exists. We very often do this, and sometimes the answer is in the affirmative. I can say that the legendary figure, King Arthur, was a really existing British monarch, that in California last summer I came upon the very mountains I have been dreaming of so persistently for years and so discovered that they really existed after all. But in doing so am I not predicating real existence of that which I have already presupposed to exist in my dreams? It might look that way, but there are less obvious features of these statements which save us from the dire consequences of that interpretation. Note that they can all be restated as a simple conjunction of two independent statements each of which is on the same level, neither presupposing the other. "King Arthur exists in legend, and King Arthur really existed in the sixth century." "Mountains of such-and-such a description exist in my dreams, and mountains of that description really exist in California." And this sort of statement gives a more faithful reflection of our intent. What we want to say is that Arthur exists both in legend and in reality, that is, we want to treat both modes of existence on a par, as having the same connection to Arthur. But on a subject-predicate interpretation this would not be the case. Real existence would be predicated of the legendary figure, but legendary existence would not be predicated of the real figure. They can be treated alike only if what we say amounts to a simple conjunction of two logically independent existential statements, whereas an admitted subject-predicate statement like "King Arthur won twelve victories" cannot be so translated. Undoubtedly there are two statements involved here, namely, "There is in legend a figure called King Arthur," and "He won twelve victories," but they are not independent. The second cannot be stated without a backward reference to the first (for the antecedent of "he"). It is this asymmetry that is the mark of the subject-predicate form. A subject-predicate statement is one with respect to which two questions must be raised. One question concerns the existence of something, and the other, concerning the applicability of an attribute to that something, cannot be raised until the first question has been answered in the affirmative. By this criterion "The legendary figure, King Arthur, really existed" is not a subject-predicate statement. We need not treat it in any such two-layered fashion.

One source of the tendency to treat "King Arthur really existed in the sixth century" as a subject-predicate statement is the strong inclination to allow such a question as "Who is it that is being said to have really existed in the sixth century?" Discussing the matter in those terms will lead us straight to the subject-predicate framework; indeed that question springs from that framework. It is the part of wisdom to recognize that the above discussion, in showing the fundamental differences between that sentence and any sentence in the subject-predicate mold, has demonstrated that the question is badly put. And having recognized that, and having seen that we can say everything we want to say without it, we must avoid it like the plague.

Thus, even admitting various modes of existence, it is impossible to construe existential statements as predicative. And yet in this more adequate perspective, the denial cannot be so clear-cut. On the standard approach (recognizing only one mode of existence) "exists" could in no way function as a predicate. But if we recognize a plurality of modes, it must be admitted that there are (rather infrequent) statements which involve something like a predicate of existence. For example, a novelist can present a character as a real man, as a character in a story, or as contained in a dream. Thus in *The Brothers Karamazov*, Ivan is a really existing man, but the Grand Inquisitor is only a figure in a dream of Ivan's. In *Tom Jones* Parson Thwackum is a real person, but Sir George Gresham only appears in a story narrated by the Man of the Hill. That is, a fictional character can, within the novel, have real, fictional, or dream existence. Again, I can dream about real people or fictional people. (By this I do not mean that the people about whom I dream can really be either real or fictional, but rather that they can be presented in the dream as either real or fictional.) Or I can dream of thinking about Eisenhower, in which case in my dream Eisenhower has existence in the understanding. In other words, among other ways of distinguishing between the characters in a novel or in a dream, we can consider the modes of existence attached to them. This gives us fictional or dream duplications of real existence, dream existence, fictional existence, and so forth. The various modes of existence, like the whole apparatus of qualities, substances, relations, and the like, are carried over bodily into fiction and dreams and exist there with all their interconnections intact. And we can put this, if we like, by saying that real existence, fictional existence, and so forth, can be predicated of a fictional or of a dream character.

But of course the possibility of this sort of predication gives no support to the thesis that existence is an attribute.

These very special sorts of statements are clearly distinguishable from ordinary statements of existence. No one would confuse our initial example about Alyosha and the Grand Inquisitor with an assertion that Alyosha really exists whereas the Grand Inquisitor does not. The heart of the denial that "exists" is a predicate is the claim that statements of existence are not predicative; this remains unshaken by the sort of predication we have just considered.

D. I have done nothing to show that "A perfect being exists" is not, or cannot be shown to be, a necessary statement; still less have I shown that there are, or can be, no necessary existential statements. Such claims are often made with great confidence, but I have never seen any conclusive arguments in their support, nor have I been able to find any. Certainly the demonstration that "exists" is not a predicate does nothing to show that no existential statements are necessary. For there are many necessary statements which turn on the logical properties of terms other than predicates, for example, the statement that if I am writing with either pen or pencil, then it is not the case that I am writing with neither pen nor pencil. The most that can be done, it seems to me, is to examine and evaluate each claim that is made for the necessity of an existential statement. This essay is designed to make a contribution to that enterprise. In it I have attempted to reveal more clearly the deficiencies in the ontological argument, and in the course of so doing to show more conclusively that "exists" is not a predicate.

10. J. N. FINDLAY (1903—)

[*J. N. Findlay, professor of philosophy in King's College, London, astonished philosophers by producing what amounts to an ontological argument for the non-existence of God. Deriving his conception of God from the Judaic-Christian tradition and insisting, with St. Anselm and other orthodox thinkers, that God, as a being worthy of worship, must be conceived as an absolutely necessary and eternal being, and one who is such that, if He exists, He must exist by His very nature and be dependent upon nothing else, Findlay argues, contrary to Leibniz, that either such a being is impossible, or the conception itself is senseless. Thus, as St. Anselm claimed to derive God's existence from the very conception of Him, Findlay claims to derive His non-existence from the very same conception.*

Replies to Findlay's provocative argument by G. E. Hughes and A. C. A. Ranier may be found in Mind, *1949.*]

CAN GOD'S EXISTENCE BE DISPROVED?[*][1]

I

The course of philosophical development has been full of attempted proofs of the existence of God. Some of these

---

[*] From *Language, Truth and Value* (1963). Reprinted by permission of the author, and the publishers: Humanities Press, Inc., New York, and George Allen & Unwin, Ltd., copyright holder.

[1] First published in *Mind*, April 1948. I have added a few words at one or two places to indicate that I think my argument holds for all who accept all that Kant says in criticism of the Ontological Proof, and not only for linguistic philosophers.

have sought a basis in the bare necessities of thought, while
others have tried to found themselves on the facts of experience. And, of these latter, some have founded themselves on *very general facts*, as that something exists, or
that something is in motion, while others have tried to
build on *highly special facts*, as that living beings are put
together in a purposive manner, or that human beings are
subject to certain improbable urges and passions, such as
the zeal for righteousness, the love for useless truths and
unprofitable beauties, as well as the many specifically religious needs and feelings. The general philosophical ver-
dict is that none of these "proofs" is truly compelling. The
proofs based on the necessities of thought are universally
regarded as fallacious: it is not thought possible to build
bridges between mere abstractions and concrete existence.
The proofs based on the general facts of existence and
motion are only felt to be valid by a minority of thinkers,
who seem quite powerless to communicate this sense of
validity to others. And while most thinkers would accord
weight to arguments resting on the special facts we have
mentioned, they wouldn't think such arguments success-
ful in ruling out a vast range of counter-possibilities. Religious people have, in fact, come to acquiesce in the total
absence of any cogent proofs of the Being they believe in:
they even find it positively satisfying that something so far
surpassing clear conception should also surpass the possibility of demonstration. And non-religious people will-
ingly mitigate their rejection with a tinge of agnosticism:
they don't so much deny the existence of God, as the existence of good reasons for believing in Him. We shall, however, maintain in this essay that there isn't room, in the
case we are examining, for all these attitudes of tentative
surmise and doubt. For we shall try to show that the Divine Existence can only be conceived, in a religiously
satisfactory manner, if we also conceive it as something
inescapable and necessary, whether for thought or reality.
From which it follows that our modern denial of necessity
or rational evidence for such an existence amounts to a
demonstration that there cannot be a God.

Before we develop this argument, we must, however,

give greater precision to our use of the term "God." For it is possible to say that there are nearly as many "Gods" as there are speakers and worshippers, and while existence may be confidently asserted or denied of *some* of them, we should feel more hesitant in the case of others. It is one thing, plainly, to pronounce on God's existence, if He be taken to be some ancient, shapeless stone, or if we identify Him with the bearded Father of the Sistine ceiling, and quite another matter, if we make of Him an "all-pervasive, immaterial intelligence," or characterize Him in some yet more negative and analogical manner. We shall, however, choose an indirect approach, and pin God down for our purposes as the "adequate object of religious attitudes."

Plainly we find it possible to gather together, under the blanket term "religious," a large range of cases of possible action, linked together by so many overlapping[2] affinities that we are ready to treat them as the varying "expressions" of a single "attitude" or "policy." And plainly we find it possible to indicate the character of that attitude by a number of descriptive phrases which, though they may err individually by savouring too strongly of particular cases, nevertheless permit us, in their totality, to draw a rough boundary round the attitude in question. Thus we might say, for instance, that a religious attitude was one in which we tended to abase ourselves before some object, to defer to it wholly, to devote ourselves to it with unquestioning enthusiasm, to bend the knee before it, whether literally or metaphorically. These phrases, and a large number of similar ones, would make perfectly plain the sort of attiude we were speaking of, and would suffice to mark it off from cognate attitudes which are much less unconditional and extreme in their tone. Clearly similar phrases would suffice to fix the boundaries of religious *feeling*. We might describe religious frames of mind as ones in which we felt ready to abase ourselves before some object, to bend the knee before it, and so forth. Here,

[2] This word is added to avoid the suggestion that there must be *one* pervasive affinity linking together all the actions commonly called "religious."

as elsewhere, we find ourselves indicating the *felt* character of our attitudes, by treating their inward character as, in some sense, a concentrated and condensed substitute for appropriate lines of action, a way of speaking that accords curiously with the functional significance of the inward.[3]

But not only do we thus incorporate, in the meanings of our various names for attitudes, a reference to this readiness for appropriate lines of action: we also incorporate in these meanings a reference to *the sorts of things or situations to which these attitudes are the normal or appropriate responses.* For, as a matter of fact, our attitudes are not indifferently evoked in *any* setting: there is a range of situations in which they normally and most readily occur. And though they may at times arise in circumstances which are not in this range, they are also readily dissipated by the consciousness that such circumstances *are* unsuitable or unusual. Thus fear is an attitude very readily evoked in situations with a character of menace or potential injury, and it is also an attitude very readily allayed by the clear perception that a given situation isn't really dangerous. And anger, likewise, in an attitude provoked very readily by perverse resistance and obstructive difficulty in some object, and is also very readily dissipated, even in animals, by the consciousness that a given object is innocent of offence. All attitudes, we may say, *presume* characters in their objects, and are, in consequence, strengthened by the discovery that their objects *have* these characters, as they are weakened by the discovery that they really haven't got them.

Not only do we find this out empirically: we also incorporate it in the *meanings* of our names for attitudes. Thus attitudes are said to be "normal," "fully justified" and so forth, if we find them altered in a certain manner (called "appropriate") by our knowledge of the actual state of things, whereas we speak of them as "queer" or "senseless" or "neurotic," if they aren't at all modified by

[3] Whatever the philosophical "ground" for it may be, this plainly is the way in which we *do* describe the "inner quality" of our felt attitudes.

this knowledge of reality. We call it abnormal, from this point of view, to feel a deep-seated fear of mice, to rage maniacally at strangers, to greet disasters with a hebephrenic giggle, whereas we think it altogether normal to deplore deep losses deeply, or to fear grave dangers gravely. And so an implicit reference to some standard object—which makes an attitude either normal or abnormal —is part of what we ordinarily mean by all our names for attitudes, and can be rendered explicit by a simple study of usage. We can consider the circumstances in which ordinary speakers would call an attitude "appropriate" or "justified."

All that philosophy achieves in this regard is merely to push further, and develop into more considered and consistent forms, the implications of such ordinary ways of speaking. It can inquire whether an attitude would still seem justified, and its object appropriate, after we had reflected long and carefully on a certain matter, and looked at it from every wonted and unwonted angle. Such consideration may lead philosophers to a different and more reasoned notion of the appropriate objects of a given attitude, than could be garnered from our unreflective ways of speaking. And these developments of ordinary usage will only seem unfeasible to victims of that strange modern confusion which thinks of attitudes exclusively as hidden processes "in our bosoms," with nothing but an adventitious relation to appropriate outward acts and objects.

II

How then may we apply these notions to the case of our religious attitudes? Plainly we shall be following the natural trends of unreflective speech if we say that religious attitudes presume *superiority* in their objects, and such superiority, moreover, as reduces us, who feel the attitudes, to comparative nothingness. For having described a worshipful attitude as one in which we feel disposed to bend the knee before some object, to defer to it wholly, and the like, we find it natural to say that such an attitude can only be fitting where the object reverenced *exceeds* us very vastly, whether in power or wisdom or in other valued qualities. While it is certainly possible to worship stocks and stones and articles of common use, one does so usually on the assumption that they aren't merely stocks and stones and ordinary articles, but the temporary seats of "indwelling presences" or centres of extraordinary powers and virtues. If one realizes clearly that such things *are* merely stocks and stones or articles of common use, one can't help suffering a total vanishing or grave abatement of religious ardour.

To feel religiously is therefore to presume surpassing greatness in some object: so much characterizes the attitudes in which we bow and bend the knee, and enters into the ordinary meaning of the word "religious". But now we advance further—in company with a large number of theologians and philosophers, who have added new touches to the portrait of deity, pleading various theoretical necessities, but really concerned to make their object worthier of our worship—and ask whether it isn't wholly anomalous to worship anything *limited* in any thinkable manner. For all limited superiorities are tainted with an obvious relativity, and can be dwarfed in thought by still mightier superiorities, in which process of being dwarfed they lose their claim upon our worshipful attitudes. And hence we are led on irresistibly to demand that our religious object should have an *unsurpassable* supremacy along all avenues, that it should tower *infinitely* above all other objects. Not only are we led to demand for it such merely quantitative superiority: we also ask that it shouldn't stand surrounded by a world of *alien* objects, which owe it no allegiance, or set limits to its influence. The proper object of religious reverence must in some manner be *all-comprehensive:* there mustn't be anything capable of existing, or of displaying any virtue, without owing all of these absolutely to this single source.

All these, certainly, are difficult requirements, involving not only the obscurities and doubtful significance of the infinite, but also all the well-worn antagonism of the immanent and transcendent, of finite sinfulness and divine perfection and preordination, which centuries of theological brooding have failed to dissipate. But we are also led on irresistibly to a yet more stringent demand, which raises difficulties which make the difficulties we have mentioned seem wholly inconsiderable: we can't help feeling that the worthy object of our worship can never be a thing that merely *happens* to exist, nor one on which all other objects merely *happen* to depend. The true object of religious reverence must not be one, merely, to which no *actual* independent realities stand opposed: it must be one to which such opposition is totally *inconceivable*. God mustn't merely cover the territory of the actual, but also, with equal comprehensiveness, the territory of the possible. And not only must the existence of *other* things be unthinkable without Him, but His own non-existence must be wholly unthinkable in any circumstances. There must, in short, be no conceivable alternative to an existence properly termed "divine": God must be wholly inescapable, as we remarked previously, whether for thought or reality. So we are led on insensibly to the barely intelligible notion of a Being in whom Essence and Existence lose their separateness. And all that the great medieval thinkers really did was to carry such a development to its logical limit.

We may, however, approach the matter from a slightly different angle. Not only is it contrary to the demands and claims inherent in religious attitudes that their object should *exist* "accidentally": it is also contrary to those demands that it should *possess its various excellences* in some merely adventitious or contingent manner. It would be quite unsatisfactory from the religious standpoint, if an object merely *happened* to be wise, good, powerful and so forth, even to a superlative degree, and if other beings had, *as a mere matter of fact,* derived their excellences from this single source. An object of this sort would doubtless deserve respect and admiration, and other quasi-religious attitudes, but it would not deserve the utter self-abandonment peculiar to the religious frame of mind. It would deserve the δουλεία canonically accorded to the saints, but not the λατρεία that we properly owe to God. We might respect this object as the crowning instance of most excellent qualities, but we should incline our head before the qualities and not before the person. Wherever such qualities were manifested, though perhaps less eminently, we should always be ready to perform an essentially similar obeisance. For though such qualities might be intimately characteristic of the Supreme Being, they still wouldn't be in any sense inalienably His own. And even if other beings had, in fact, derived such qualities from this sovereign source, they still would be *their own* qualities, possessed by them in their own right. We should have no better reason to *adore* the author of such virtues, than sons have reason to adore superior parents, or pupils to adore superior teachers. For while these latter may deserve deep deference, the fact that we are coming to *participate* in their excellences renders them unworthy of our *worship*. Plainly a being that possesses and imparts desirable qualities—which other things might nevertheless have manifested though this source were totally absent—has all the utter inadequacy as a religious object which is expressed by saying that it would be *idolatrous* to worship it. Wisdom, kindness and other excellences deserve respect wherever they are manifested, but no being can appropriate them as its personal perquisites, even if it does possess them in a superlative degree. And so we are led on irresistibly, by the demands inherent in religious reverence, to hold that an adequate object of our worship must possess its various qualities *in some necessary manner*. These qualities must be intrinsically incapable of belonging to anything except in so far as they belong primarily to the object of our worship. Again we are led on to a queer and barely intelligible Scholastic doctrine, that God isn't merely good, but is in some manner indistinguishable from His own (and anything else's) goodness.

III

What, however, are the consequences of these requirements for the possibility of God's existence? Plainly (for all who share a contemporary outlook) they entail not only that there isn't a God, but that the Divine Existence is either senseless[4] or impossible. The modern mind feels not the faintest axiomatic force in principles which trace contingent things back to some necessarily existent source, nor does it find it hard to conceive that things should display various excellent qualities without deriving them from a source which manifests them supremely. Those who believe in necessary truths which aren't merely tautological, think that such truths merely connect the *possible* instances of various characteristics with each other: they don't expect such truths to tell them whether there *will* be instances of any characteristics. This is the outcome of the whole medieval and Kantian criticism of the Ontological Proof. And, on a yet more modern view of the matter, necessity in propositions merely reflects our use of words, the arbitrary conventions of our language. On such a view the Divine Existence could only be a necessary matter if we had made up our minds to speak theistically *whatever the empirical circumstances might turn out to be*. This, doubtless, would suffice for some, who speak theistically, much as Spinoza spoke monistically, merely to give expression to a particular way of looking at things, or of feeling about them. It would also suffice for those who make use of the term "God" to cover whatever tendencies towards righteousness and beauty are actually included in the make-up of our world. But it wouldn't suffice for the full-blooded worshipper, who can't help finding our actual world anything but edifying, and its half-formed tendencies towards righteousness and beauty very far from adorable.

The religious frame of mind seems, in fact, to be in a quandary; it seems invincibly determined both to eat its cake and have it. It desires the Divine Existence both to have that inescapable character which can, on Kantian or modern views, only be found where truth reflects a connection of characteristics or an arbitrary convention, and also the character of "making a real difference" which is only possible where truth doesn't have this merely hypothetical or linguistic basis. We may accordingly deny that

[4] I have included this alternative, of which I am not fond, merely because so many modern thinkers make use of it in this sort of connection.

these approaches allow us to remain agnostically poised in regard to God: they force us to come down on the atheistic side. For if God is to satisfy religious claims and needs, He must be a being in every way inescapable, One whose existence and whose possession of certain excellences we cannot possibly conceive away. And the views in question really make it self-evidently absurd (if they don't make it ungrammatical) to speak of such a Being and attribute existence to Him. It was indeed an ill day for Anselm when he hit upon his famous proof. For on that day he not only laid bare something that is of the essence of an adequate religious object, but also something that entails its necessary non-existence.[5]

The force of our argument must not, however, be exaggerated. We haven't proved that there aren't beings of all degrees of excellence and greatness, who may deserve attitudes approximating indefinitely to religious reverence. But such beings will at best be instances of valued qualities which we too may come to exemplify, though in lesser degree. Not only would it be idolatrous for us to worship them, but it would also be monstrous for them to exact worship, or to care for it. The attitude of such beings to our reverence would necessarily be deprecating: they would prefer co-operative atheists to adoring zealots. And they would probably hide themselves like royal personages from the anthems of their worshippers, and perhaps the fact that there are so few positive signs of their presence is itself a feeble evidence of their real existence. But whether such beings exist or not, they are not divine, and can never satisfy the demands inherent in religious reverence. The effect of our argument will further be to discredit generally such forms of religion as attach a uniquely sacred meaning to existent things, whether these things be men or acts or institutions or writings.

But there are other frames of mind, to which we shouldn't deny the name "religious," which acquiesce quite readily in the non-existence of their objects. (This non-existence might, in fact, be taken to be the "real

[5] Or "non-significance," if this alternative is preferred.

meaning" of saying that religious objects and realities are "not of this world.") In such frames of mind we give ourselves over unconditionally and gladly to the task of indefinite approach toward a certain imaginary focus[6] where nothing actually is, and we find this task sufficiently inspiring and satisfying without demanding (absurdly) that there should be something actual at that limit. And the atheistic religious attitude we have mentioned has also undergone reflective elaboration by such philosophers as Fichte and Erigena and Alexander. There is, then, a religious atheism which takes full stock of our arguments, and we may be glad that this is so. For since the religious spirit is one of reverence before things greater than ourselves, we should be gravely impoverished and arrested if this spirit ceased to be operative in our personal and social life. It would certainly be better that this spirit should survive, with all its fallacious existential trimmings, than that we should cast it forth merely in order to be rid of such irrelevances.

[In the Introduction to *Language, Mind and Value*, published fifteen years later, Findlay comments as follows on this essay:]

. . . I still think that it makes a valid point: that if it is *possible*, in some logical and not merely epistemological sense, that there is no God, then God's existence is not merely doubtful but *impossible*, since nothing *capable* of non-existence could be a God at all. Kant, who at times suggested that the existence of anything was a synthetic and *a posteriori* matter (though perhaps establishable only by a non-sensuous intuition) should have seen that his views constituted a *disproof* of the existence of God, not left Him a flawless ideal to which some noumenal reality *might* correspond. Professor Hartshorne has, however, convinced me that my argument permits a ready inversion, and that one can very well argue that if God's existence is in any way *possible*, then it is also *certain* and *necessary* that God exists, a position which should give some comfort

[6] To use a Kantian comparison.

to the shade of Anselm. The notion of God, like the notion of the class of all classes not members of themselves, has plainly unique logical properties, and I do not now think that my article finally *decides* how we should cope with such uniqueness.

11. CHARLES HARTSHORNE (1897–   )

[*A professor of philosophy at the University of Texas, Charles Hartshorne is a leading proponent of the ontological argument and has probably written more extensively on it than has any other contemporary philosopher. Indeed,* Man's Vision of God, *the book from which this selection is taken, is devoted entirely to that argument. Hartshorne distinguishes two lines of argument in Anselm, maintaining that the traditional criticism of the ontological argument holds against only one of them, leaving the other unscathed.*]

THE NECESSARILY EXISTENT*

Where would such an idea, say as that of God, come from, if not from direct experience? . . . No: as to God, open your eyes—and your heart, which is also a perceptive organ—and you see him. But you may ask, Don't you admit there are any delusions? Yes: I may think a thing is black, and on close examination it may turn out to be bottle-green. But I cannot think a thing is black if there is no such thing as black. Neither can I think that a certain action is self-sacrificing, if no such thing as self-sacrifice exists, although it may be very rare. It is the nominalists, and the nominalists alone, who indulge in such skepticism, which the scientific method utterly condemns.

CHARLES SANDERS PEIRCE,
in *Collected Papers*, Vol. VI

* From *Man's Vision of God* (1941). Harper & Row, Inc., Publishers. Reprinted by permission of the author.

The ontological argument turns logically upon the unique relation between the possibility and the actuality, the "essence" and the "existence," of God. With ordinary finite ideas the task of knowledge is to decide among three cases: (1) the type of thing conceived is impossible, and hence non-existent (e.g., a moral being totally without "freedom"); (2) the type of thing is possible, but there is no actual example (a Euclidean space?); (3) the thing is possible, and there is an example (a speaking animal). The ontological argument holds that with the idea of God only two of these three cases need be considered, since one of the three, (2), is meaningless. If, the argument holds, there exists no God, then there also can be no possibility of the existence of a God, and the concept is nonsense, like that of "round square." If, further, it can be shown that the idea of God is not nonsensical, that it must have an at least possible object, then it follows that it has an actual object, since a "merely possible" God is, if the argument is sound, inconceivable. *Where impossibility and mere unactualized possibility are both excluded, there nothing remains but actuality, if the idea has any meaning at all.*

The ontological argument itself does not suffice to exclude the impossibility or meaninglessness of God, but only to exclude his mere possibility. Or, as Leibniz said, it must assume that God is not impossible. (We shall consider presently whether the argument can be extended so as to justify this assumption.) The inventor of the argument, Anselm, took it for granted that the man with religious experience, to whom he addressed his discourse, though he may doubt God's existence, will not easily doubt that in hoping that there is a God he is at least hoping for something with a self-consistent meaning. Now, given a meaning, there must be something which is meant. We do not think just our act of thinking. What we think may not be actual, but can it be less than possible—unless it be a self-contradictory combination of factors, singly and separately possible? In short, when we think, can we fail to refer to something beyond our thought which, either as a whole or in its elements, is at least possible? Granting this, the ontological argument says that, with reference to God, "at least possible" is indistinguishable from "possible *and* actual" (though, as we shall see, "possible" here means simply "not impossible" and has no positive content different from actuality). Let us now present the reasons for the contention that "at least possible" and "actual" are indistinguishable in the case of the divine.

According to one theory of possibility, a given type of entity is possible if the most general features, the strictly generic characters, of existence or of the universe are compatible with the production of such an entity. Thus, there is no contradiction of the most general features of reality in the supposition that nature has really produced Mr. Micawber. There is contradiction of the details of nature (such as the detail that Micawber is a character in a novel written by a highly imaginative author), but these may be supposed otherwise without destroying the meaning, the generic content, of "existence." But the idea of God is the idea of a being everlasting in duration, and independent, in a certain aspect of his being (in his individual "essence"), from everything else. Such a being could not be produced, since he must then be both derivative and underivative, everlasting and yet not everlasting. To create the omniscient, one must endow him with a perfect memory of the past before he existed; to create the omnipotent, one must endow him with incomparably more power, a metaphysically different order of power, than that which created him. It is hardly necessary to prolong the discussion: no theologian holding either type-one or type-two theism has ever rejected that portion of the ontological argument which consists in the proof that *God could not be a mere possibility;* and (as we are about to show) it is demonstrable that in order to reject this proof one must construct a theory of possibility which would not be required for ordinary purposes, so that the tables may be turned upon those who accuse the argument of making God an exception to all principles of knowledge. The argument does make God an exception, but only in the sense that it *deduces* this exceptional status from a generally applicable theory of possibility together with the definition of

God. Nothing else is required. The opposition, on the contrary, sets up a general principle which, but for God and the desire to avoid asserting his existence (as following from his possibility), would be without merit.

It might, however, be thought that "possible" need not mean the consistency of the supposition of the thing's being produced, or of its coming into existence due to some cause. Only with one type of thing, it may be held, does "possible" mean this. With another type, consisting of things with universal extent in time, a thing either just always exists or just always lacks existence, either status being possible, although no temporal cause could conceivably effect the difference.

I submit that this is a view so paradoxical that it would hardly be considered at all but for two reasons. One is that it invalidates the ontological argument. The other is that it lends color to the supposition that the laws of nature discoverable by science are eternal laws, although their non-existence is logically possible, and although, as eternal, they could never have been produced, constituting, as they do, the very machinery of all production, the presupposition of all events. The alternative to this supposition about laws is the idea that the laws of nature with which physics deals are themselves produced by the cosmic process, the most general principles of which are beyond "law" in this sense. (There must be some sort of law governing the production of laws, but this higher law is of another order, and may be conceived as the aesthetic principle of the value of order as such, and of the no less real value of a certain element of freedom and disorder, of surprise and novelty, as well as repetition and predictability.) On this view, nothing is possible and at the same time not actual unless at some stage of the cosmic evolution the forces were such that there is no contradiction in the idea of their having taken a turn which sooner or later would have led to the production of the thing in question. Thus, if nature had developed other habits—and who shall say she could not have?—other "laws" would have obtained. But clearly God could not be possible in this way, and he is the *only consistently conceivable object which must be conceived as unproduced,* a reality always existing or never existing or even capable of existing, either in essence uncaused or a mere nonentity.

The old objection that if a perfect being must exist then a perfect island or a perfect devil must exist is not perhaps very profound. For it is answered simply by denying that anyone can conceive perfection, in the strict sense employed by the argument, to be possessed by an island or a devil. A perfect devil would have at the same time to be infinitely responsible for all that exists besides itself, and yet infinitely averse to all that exists. It would have to attend with unrivaled care and patience and fullness of realization to the lives of all other beings (which must depend for existence upon this care), and yet it must hate all these things with matchless bitterness. It must savagely torture a cosmos every item of which is integral with its own being, united to it with a vivid intimacy such as we can only dimly imagine. In short, whether a perfect God is sense or nonsense, a perfect devil is unequivocally nonsense, and it is of no import whether the nonsensical does or does not necessarily exist, since in any case it necessarily does not exist, and its existence would be nothing, even though a necessary nothing. Clearly, again, an island is not in essence unproducible and self-sufficient. Of course one can arbitrarily put concepts together and suppose that an island which could never be destroyed and had never been produced would be better than one capable of production, since some form of eternal life might go on upon it, undisturbed by any possibility of an end to such a world. But it is not apparent what would make such a world an island, if the "waters" which "washed" it never wore its shores, and if it were not a part of the surface of a body in space surrounded by other bodies capable of smashing it to pieces, and were not composed of particles capable of ultimately separating, etc. The question is if such a conception would in the end be distinguishable from the idea of the cosmos as the perpetually renewed body of God, that is, not an island in the least, but an aspect of the very idea of God whose self-existence is upheld by the argument.

The question is, Can a possibility be real, unless it would, *if* actual, be an effect of a cause which is real, or the effect of a possible cause which, if actual, would itself be the effect of a cause which . . . (the series ultimately terminating in a cause which is real)? Otherwise, possibility is something wholly apart from actuality, something no experience could ever reveal or evidence support.

I may be told that "logical possibility" is simply self-consistency and that no further reality than this consistency is required. But the reply is that the meanings whose consistency is granted must mean something, and this referent of the meanings is not the consistency but the presupposition of there being any meanings, consistent or otherwise. If a consistent meaning means something, but something not even possible, then it means something very odd indeed. If it means only its own consistency, then it is really meaningless.

Let us be empirical. I may think of any object of any color I choose; will it be denied that an object of this color is consistently conceivable as a production of "nature"? In fact, of course, objects of at least approximately the same color have been actually given in my experience. The step "from thought to reality" is merely the reverse reading of the step from reality to thought without which there is no thought, as the very logicians who attack the ontological argument on the ground that it seeks to "derive existence from a mere idea" would be the first to grant. We are always in contact with the forces which produce realities, and hence we can think both actual and possible objects. Or, in other terms, we can distinguish, in the reality some portion of which is always given to us, between the essential or generic features and the details, and can see that this distinction implies that mutually incompatible details are both or all compatible (separately, though not together) with the generic features. But God is not a detail, and only contradiction results from trying to make his possibility conceivable in the fashion in which alone mere possibility is ever really conceived.

We may go further. The reason God is not a detail, whose existence would be one of two equally conceivable alternatives, is that he is really the content of "existence," the generic factor of the universe. To conceive God is not to conceive what might exist, but what "existence" itself must be—if the idea of God is not meaningless. Either God is nothing at all, or all else that exists exists in and through him, and therefore contingently, and he himself exists (in his essence, though not in his accidents) solely in and through himself, that is, necessarily. The cosmological argument showed that only "God" makes clearly conceivable the flexibility of the generic features of existence by which alternative details of existence can, as alternatives, be real. Alternativeness is one way of looking at creativeness, and the essential or cosmic creativeness is the divine, and nothing else.

Thus to make God's existence exceptional in relation to his conceivability is a result, not a violation, of the general principle of existence. Whatever is merely possible, this possibility as such is real, is other than nothing, only thanks to something which itself is not merely possible but is reality itself as self-identical, or as that which, being the ground of possibility, is more than merely possible. It is an implication of the idea of God that he *is* that ground.

At some point potentiality and actuality must touch, and at some point meaning must imply existence. God is the general, the cosmic and everlasting, the essential or a priori case of the unity of essence and existence, and he is this because he is supreme potentiality as existing power, a real agent who eternally does one or other of various pairs of alternatives which he "can" do. All meaning implicitly asserts God, because all meaning is nothing less than a reference to one or other of the two aspects of the cosmic reality, what it *has* done or what it *could* do—that is, to the consequent or primordial natures of God.

It has been objected to the ontological argument that existence is not a predicate, and hence cannot be implied by the predicate "perfection." But if existence is not a predicate, yet the *mode* of a thing's existence—its contingency or necessity of existence—is included in every predicate whatever. To be an atom is essentially to be a contingent product of forces which were also capable of not producing the atom, and doubtless for long ages did not do so. Again, contingent existence (the equal compatibility with existence or its negative) is implied by such predicates as those describing a man. His weaknesses imply that it is not true that he is the master of existence, able to exist through his own resources. The strength of God implies the opposite relation to existence. "Self-existence" is a predicate which necessarily and uniquely belongs to God, for it is part of the predicate divinity. It is part of the nature of ordinary causes that they are themselves effects of causes which antedate them. It is part of the nature of supreme causality that it is coextensive in time with all causal action. (Not that God's action is in no sense affected by causes, for the law of action and reaction may apply to God; but simply that God, as an individual, cannot have originated out of pre-existent individuals. His existence is uncaused, whether or not all his properties are. Or, otherwise expressed, his essential properties, being one with his existence, have no ground in other individuals; but he may be subject, in spite of the Thomists, to accidents whose explanation is in part to be sought in the accidents occurring in other individuals.) To be God is essentially to be the supreme productive force itself, unproduced and unproducible (except in its accidents) by any force whatsoever. Hence either God is actual, or there is nothing which could be meant by his possible existence. Thus that God's essence should imply his existential status (as contingent or necessary) is not an exception to the rule, but an example of it, since the rule is that contingency or non-contingency of existence follows from the kind of thing in question.

There is another way in which the argument illustrates rather than violates general principles. The argument is not that God's individual nature implies his existence, while other individual natures do not. It may reasonably be held that every individual nature implies existence, and indeed is an existence. By regarding possibilities alone, one can never reach any truly individual character. Individuation and actualization are inseparable by any test, since individuals as such are known only by pointing. Description of contingent things gives always a class quality, unless in the description is included some reference to the space-time world which itself is identified as "this" world, not by description. But "perfection," as we shall see presently, is the one description which defines no class, not even a "one-membered" one, but either nothing or else an individual. If, then, it is true, as it seems to be, that mere possibility is always a matter of class, then the perfect being, which is no class, is either impossible or actual— there being no fourth status.

But if every individual quality implies existence, must not all individuals exist necessarily? The answer is that contingency is not a relation of existence to a thing, but of a thing to existence. To say a thing might not exist is not to say there might be the thing without existence. It is rather to say there might be existence without the thing. To pass from the actual to what might be is to generalize, ultimately to refer to the uttermost generalities. It is the world (in its generic features) which does not imply its contingent inhabitants, not the inhabitants which do not imply the world with themselves as its existing parts. They do imply it. Without it they, as individuals, would not be, even as possible. There is an unutilized possibility of individuals, but not an individuality of the unutilized possibility. Mr. Micawber is a quasi-individual, with some of the aesthetic properties of an individual, but not an individual in the strict sense. He is a class, specific enough to simulate an individual for the purposes of the aesthetic illusion or "make-believe."

The unique status of God is that no distinction can be drawn between any individual having perfection and any other. Every perfect being must have the same space-time locus (omnipresence), and must know the same things— all there are to know. If there had been another world, the God of this our world would have known it, for the very possibility of another world can be related to God only as something *he* (not some other God) could have done or can still do. Hence "the perfect" is no class of possibilities, all of which might be unactual, but only an individual character belonging to nothing, not even potentially (for the only individuality that could be involved is already involved), or else belonging to the one real perfect individual.

The necessary being is, then, that individual which existence implies, and which itself implies, not simply existence (for every individual does that), but implies, through the identity of its generic with its individual character, that (so far as its primordial nature is concerned) there is in its case no separation between possibility and actuality, the class and the individual. In other words, "perfection" implies that existence itself necessarily contains a real perfection, or that existence, in its cosmically essential features, *is* perfection as existent, as the unity of being and possibility. Or, perfection implies that existence, any and all existence, implies the existence of perfection as its ground.

Again, to conceive a thing in two alternative states, actual and possible, is to conceive something common to these two states, as well as something different. But between the world with God and the world without God no common feature could be found. For the world with God is the world completely dependent upon the existence of God, for both its actuality and its possibility, and hence it follows that in the absence of God nothing of the world as it would be with God could be identified.

Doubtless these are all ways of construing the one simple principle: nothing but existent perfection could make perfection possible, or rather, perfection cannot have the dependent relation to other things implied by the status of mere possibility, but must have either the status of an impossible idea or pseudo-idea, or else must be simply actual, with no alternative of non-actual possibility at all.

If it be thought suspicious that the ontological argument argues from a unique relation of God to existence (though one deduced from the normal relation plus the definition of perfection), let it be remembered that, by definition, God's relation to every question is unique. He is the unique being, unique because maximal, the only unsurpassed and unsurpassable being (in senses A and R). Naturally, God's relation to existence is maximal also, that is, he exists under all possible circumstances, times, and places, in other words, necessarily. That which would exist, if at all, necessarily, cannot be non-existent and yet possible, for this would mean having existence as a contingent alternative, and a contingent alternative cannot be necessary. To object to this is to object to the idea of God, and not merely to the affirmation, "There is a being corresponding to the idea."

If all individuals are contingent, then the whole of existence is contingent, and it might be that nothing existed, or it might be true (though nonsensical) that there was nothing of which any proposition would be true. Furthermore, what could constitute the identity of existence as such, if not an eternal and necessary individual manifested in all individuals? We human beings tend to carry our own personality with us in all our hypotheses, in so far as we say to ourselves, Suppose *I* were to experience so and so. This gives an aspect of identity by which we might try to define existence as such. But the definition would be solipsistic. Hence there must be some further aspect of identity, like ourselves in being a concrete existent, but unlike us in being able to constitute the unity, the all-embracing register of existence itself, without limitation upon conceivable variety and independence. This is what God is, the all-embracing register of existence, perfect in his flexible and tolerant ("merciful") sensitivity to all experiences, who can see things as they see themselves, also as other things see them, and also as they are related without distinct awareness on the part either of themselves or of other imperfect things.

It is to the credit of the ontological argument that it has to be opposed by making an absolute disjunction between meaning and its referent, reality, or between universals and individuals, a disjunction *at no point* mediated by a higher principle. Only if there is *one* actual individual whose presence is universal, have universals an intelligible ground in actuality. Otherwise we have to relate mere universals and mere individuals by—what? Ordinary individuals, being non-universal in their relevance, cannot explain the identity of the universals as such. Aristotelian objections to disembodied universals can be sustained only

if there be a universal embodiment, a "concrete" universal
so far as present actuality is concerned, though a universal
which is also (contrary to Hegelianism) abstract so far as
the future and potentiality are involved.

Thus there is not from any point of view good reason to
object to the exceptional status of God's existence, every
reason to welcome it as the completion of the theory of
meaning.

It is often said (and with an air of great wisdom) that
a "mere idea" cannot reach existence, that only experience
can do that. But there is no absolute disjunction between
thought and experience. A thought *is* an experience of a
certain kind, it means *through* experience, even when it
reaches only a possibility. A thought which does not mean
by virtue of an experience is simply a thought which does
not mean. Therefore, if we have a meaning for our thought
of God, we also have experience of him, whether experience of him as possible or as actual being the question.
It is too late to assert total lack of experience, once meaning has been granted. The only doubt can be whether the
experience, already posited, is such as to establish possibility only, or existence also. But in the case of God no
distinction between "not-impossible" and "actual" can be
experienced or conceived. Hence we have only to exclude
impossibility or meaninglessness to establish actuality.

Moreover, since God is conceived as all-pervasive of actuality and possibility, if we do not know God as existent,
it cannot be because we have been denied some requisite
special experience, since either *any* experience is sufficient,
or else none could possibly be. Or, once more, either God
is a meaningless term or there exists a divine being.

In still other words: either the idea of God is less than
an idea, or it is more than a "mere idea" such as might
designate an unactualized possibility, and is a direct awareness of an actual deity—as not only the mystics, but most
theologians, have maintained. "Deity" may be nonsense,
but a mere idea it cannot, without nonsense, be. To para-
phrase Kant's final remark on the subject, all disputation
about this, the real, point of the ontological argument is
labor lost, as much as disputation about arithmetic. To

say God cannot be a mere potency and to say two and two cannot make five differ in the degree of clearness of the ideas involved, but not in the a priori, or (relatively) self-evident, character of the reasoning.

That the ontological argument is hypothetical we have admitted. It says, "*If* 'God' stands for something conceivable, it stands for something actual." But this hypothetical character is often distorted out of all recognition. We are told that the only logical relation brought out by the argument is this: The necessary being, if it exists, exists necessarily. Thus to be able to use the argument in order to conclude "God exists necessarily," we should have to know the premise "God exists." This makes the argument seem ludicrous enough, but it is itself based on a self-contradictory assumption, which says, "If the necessary being happens to exist, that is, if as mere contingent fact, it exists, then it exists not as contingent fact, but as necessary truth." Instead of this nonsense, we must say, "If the phrase 'necessary being' has a meaning, then what it means exists necessarily, and if it exists necessarily, then, a fortiori, it exists." The "if" in the statement, "if it exists, it exists necessarily," cannot have the force of making the existence of the necessary being contingent—except in the sense that the argument leaves it open to suppose that the phrase "necessary being" is nonsense, and of course nonsense has no objective referent, possible or actual. Thus, what we should maintain is, "that which exists, if at all, necessarily," is the same as "that which is conceivable, if at all, only if it exists." Granting that it is conceivable, it then follows that it exists because it could not, being an object of thought at all, be a non-actual object. Or once more, the formula might be this: The necessary being, if it is not nothing, and therefore the object of no possible positive idea, is actual.

12. NORMAN MALCOLM (1911–   )

[*Norman Malcolm, professor of philosophy at Cornell University, has produced one of the clearest and most striking defenses of St. Anselm in recent philosophical literature. Like Hartshorne, Malcolm distinguishes two lines of thought in St. Anselm's* Proslogion, *the first of which he considers to be essentially that which Descartes subsequently set forth, but the other more uniquely scholastic. The first line of thought Malcolm rejects as inconclusive, agreeing with Kant, but the second, which purports to establish not merely the existence, but the necessary existence, of God, Malcolm considers correct.*]

A. MALCOLM'S STATEMENT OF ANSELM'S ONTOLOGICAL ARGUMENTS*

I believe that in Anselm's *Proslogion* and *Responsio editoris* there are two different pieces of reasoning which he did not distinguish from one another, and that a good deal of light may be shed on the philosophical problem of "the ontological argument" if we do distinguish them. In Chapter 2 of the *Proslogion*[1] Anselm says that we believe that God is *something a greater than which cannot be con-*

* From *The Philosophical Review*, Vol. LXIX (1960). Reprinted by permission of the author and the Editorial Board of *The Philosophical Review*.

[1] I have consulted the Latin text of the *Proslogion*, of *Gaunilonis Pro Insipiente*, and of the *Responsio editoris*, in S. Anselmi, *Opera Omnia*, edited by F. C. Schmitt (Secovii, 1938), vol. I. With numerous modifications, I have used the English translation by S. N. Deane: *St. Anselm* (La Salle, Illinois, 1948).

ceived. (The Latin is *aliquid quo nihil maius cogitari possit.* Anselm sometimes uses the alternative expressions *aliquid quo maius nihil cogitari potest, id quo maius cogitari nequit, aliquid quo maius cogitari non valet.*) Even the fool of the Psalm who says in his heart there is no God, when he hears this very thing that Anselm says, namely, "something a greater than which cannot be conceived," understands what he hears, and what he understands is in his understanding though he does not understand that it exists.

Apparently Anselm regards it as tautological to say that whatever is understood is in the understanding (*quidquid intelligitur in intellectu est*): he uses *intelligitur* and *in intellectu est* as interchangeable locutions. The same holds for another formula of his: whatever is thought is in thought (*quidquid cogitatur in cogitatione est*).[2]

Of course many things may exist in the understanding that do not exist in reality; for example, elves. Now, says Anselm, something a greater than which cannot be conceived exists in the understanding. But it cannot exist *only* in the understanding, for to exist in reality is greater. Therefore that thing a greater than which cannot be conceived cannot exist only in the understanding, for then a greater thing could be conceived: namely, one that exists both in the understanding and in reality.[3]

Here I have a question. It is not clear to me whether Anselm means that (a) existence in reality by itself is greater than existence in the understanding, or that (b) existence in reality and existence in the understanding together are greater than existence in the understanding alone. Certainly he accepts (b). But he might also accept (a), as Descartes apparently does in *Meditation III* when

[2] See *Proslogion* 1 and *Responsio* 2.
[3] Anselm's actual words are: "Et certe id quo maius cogitari nequit, non potest esse in solo intellectu. Si enim vel in solo intellectu est, potest cogitari esse et in re, quod maius est. Si ergo id quo maius cogitari non potest, est in solo intellectu: id ipsum quo maius cogitari non potest, est quo maius cogitari potest. Sed certe hoc esse non potest." *Proslogion* 2.

he suggests that the mode of being by which a thing is "objectively in the understanding" is *imperfect*.[4] Of course Anselm might accept both (a) and (b). He might hold that in general something is greater if it has both of these "modes of existence" than if it has either one alone, but also that existence in reality is a more perfect mode of existence than existence in the understanding.

In any case, Anselm holds that something is greater if it exists both in the understanding and in reality than if it exists merely in the understanding. An equivalent way of putting this interesting proposition, in a more current terminology, is: something is greater if it is both conceived of and exists than if it is merely conceived of. Anselm's reasoning can be expressed as follows: *id quo maius cogitari nequit* cannot be merely conceived of and not exist, for then it would not be *id quo maius cogitari nequit*. The doctrine that something is greater if it exists in addition to being conceived of, than if it is only conceived of, could be called the doctrine that *existence is a perfection*. Descartes maintained, in so many words, that existence is a perfection,[5] and presumably he was holding Anselm's doctrine, although he does not, in *Meditation V* or elsewhere, argue in the way that Anselm does in *Proslogion 2*.

When Anselm says, "And certainly, that than which nothing greater can be conceived cannot exist merely in the understanding. For suppose it exists merely in the understanding, then it can be conceived to exist in reality, which is greater,"[6] he is claiming that if I conceived of a being of great excellence, that being would be *greater* (more excellent, more perfect) if it existed than if it did not exist. His supposition that "it exists merely in the understanding" is the supposition that it is conceived of but does not exist. Anselm repeated this claim in his reply to the criticism of the monk Gaunilo. Speaking of the being a greater than which cannot be conceived, he says:

---

[4] Haldane and Ross, *The Philosophical Works of Descartes*, 2 vols. (Cambridge, 1931), I, 163.

[5] *Op. cit.*, p. 182.

[6] *Proslogion* 2; Deane, p. 8.

I have said that if it exists merely in the understanding it can be conceived to exist in reality, which is greater. Therefore, if it exists merely in the understanding obviously the very being a greater than which cannot be conceived, is one a greater than which can be conceived. What, I ask, can follow better than that? For if it exists merely in the understanding, can it not be conceived to exist in reality? And if it can be so conceived does not he who conceives of this conceive of a thing greater than it, if it does exist merely in the understanding? Can anything follow better than this: that if a being a greater than which cannot be conceived exists merely in the understanding, it is something a greater than which can be conceived? What could be plainer?[7]

He is implying, in the first sentence, that if I conceive of something which does not exist then it is possible for it to exist, and *it will be greater if it exists than if it does not exist.*

The doctrine that existence is a perfection is remarkably queer. It makes sense and is true to say that my future house will be a better one if it is insulated than if it is not insulated; but what could it mean to say that it will be a better house if it exists than if it does not? My future child will be a better man if he is honest than if he is not; but who would understand the saying that he will be a better man if he exists than if he does not? Or who understands the saying that if God exists He is more perfect than if He does not exist? One might say, with some intelligibility, that it would be better (for oneself or for mankind) if God exists than if He does not—but that is a different matter.

A king might desire that his next chancellor should have knowledge, wit, and resolution; but it is ludicrous to add that the king's desire is to have a chancellor who exists. Suppose that two royal councilors, A and B, were asked to draw up separately descriptions of the most perfect chancellor they could conceive, and that the descriptions they produced were identical except that A included existence in his list of attributes of a perfect chancellor and B did not. (I do not mean that B put nonexistence in his list.) One and the same person could satisfy both descriptions. More to the point, any person who satisfied A's description would *necessarily* satisfy B's description and *vice versa!* This is to say that A and B did not produce descriptions that differed in any way but rather one and the same description of necessary and desirable qualities in a chancellor. A only made a show of putting down a desirable quality that B had failed to include.

I believe I am merely restating an observation that Kant made in attacking the notion that "existence" or "being" is a "real predicate." He says:

> By whatever and by however many predicates we may think a thing—even if we completely determine it—we do not make the least addition to the thing when we further declare that this thing *is*. Otherwise, it would not be exactly the same thing that exists, but something more than we had thought in the concept; and we could not, therefore, say that the exact object of my concept exists.[8]

Anselm's ontological proof of *Proslogion* 2 is fallacious because it rests on the false doctrine that existence is a perfection (and therefore that "existence" is a "real predicate"). It would be desirable to have a rigorous refutation of the doctrine but I have not been able to provide one. I am compelled to leave the matter at the more or less intuitive level of Kant's observation. In any case, I believe that the doctrine does not belong to Anselm's other formulation of the ontological argument. It is worth noting that Gassendi anticipated Kant's criticism when he said, against Descartes:

> Existence is a perfection neither in God nor in anything else; it is rather that in the absence of which there is no perfection. . . . Hence neither is existence held to exist in a thing in the way that perfections

[8] *The Critique of Pure Reason,* tr. by Norman Kemp Smith (London, 1929), p. 505.

do, nor if the thing lacks existence is it said to be imperfect (or deprived of a perfection), so much as to
be nothing.[9]

II

I take up now the consideration of the second ontological proof, which Anselm presents in the very next chapter
of the *Proslogion*. (There is no evidence that he thought of
himself as offering two different proofs.) Speaking of the
being a greater than which cannot be conceived, he says:

> And it so truly exists that it cannot be conceived not
> to exist. For it is possible to conceive of a being which
> cannot be conceived not to exist; and this is greater
> than one which can be conceived not to exist. Hence,
> if that, than which nothing greater can be conceived,
> can be conceived not to exist, it is not that than which
> nothing greater can be conceived. But this is a con-
> tradiction. So truly, therefore, is there something than
> which nothing greater can be conceived, that it can-
> not even be conceived not to exist.
> And this being thou art, O Lord, our God.[10]

Anselm is saying two things: first, that a being whose non-
existence is logically impossible is "greater" than a being
whose nonexistence is logically possible (and therefore
that a being a greater than which cannot be conceived
must be one whose nonexistence is logically impossible);
second, that *God* is a being than which a greater cannot
be conceived.

In regard to the second of these assertions, there certainly is *a* use of the word "God," and I think far the more
common use, in accordance with which the statements
"God is the greatest of all beings," "God is the most perfect
being," "God is the supreme being," are *logically* necessary truths, in the same sense that the statement "A square
has four sides" is a logically necessary truth. If there is a

[9] Haldane and Ross, II, 186.
[10] *Proslogion* 3; Deane, pp. 8–9.

man named "Jones" who is the tallest man in the world, the statement "Jones is the tallest man in the world" is merely true and is not a logically necessary truth. It is a virtue of Anselm's unusual phrase, "a being a greater than which cannot be conceived,"[11] to make it explicit that the sentence "God is the greatest of all beings" expresses a logically necessary truth and not a mere matter of fact such as the one we imagined about Jones.

With regard to Anselm's first assertion (namely, that a being whose nonexistence is logically impossible is greater than a being whose nonexistence is logically possible) perhaps the most puzzling thing about it is the use of the word "greater." It appears to mean exactly the same as "superior," "more excellent," "more perfect." This equivalence by itself is of no help to us, however, since the latter expressions would be equally puzzling here. What is required is some explanation of their use.

We do think of *knowledge,* say, as an excellence, a good thing. If A has more knowledge of algebra than B we express this in common language by saying that A has a *better* knowledge of algebra than B, or that A's knowledge of algebra is *superior* to B's, whereas we should not say that B has a better or superior *ignorance* of algebra than A. We do say "greater ignorance," but here the word "greater" is used purely quantitatively.

Previously I rejected *existence* as a perfection. Anselm is maintaining in the remarks last quoted, not that existence is a perfection, but that *the logical impossibility of nonexistence is a perfection.* In other words, *necessary existence* is a perfection. His first ontological proof uses the principle that a thing is greater if it exists than if it does not exist. His second proof employs the different principle that a thing is greater if it necessarily exists than if it does not necessarily exist.

[11] Professor Robert Calhoun has pointed out to me that a similar locution had been used by Augustine. In *De moribus Manichaeorum* (Bk. II, ch. xi, sec. 24), he says that God is a being *quo esse aut cogitari melius nihil possit* (*Patrologiae Patrum Latinorum,* ed. by J. P. Migne, Paris, 1841–1845, vol. 32: *Augustinus,* vol. 1).

Some remarks about the notion of *dependence* may help to make this latter principle intelligible. Many things depend for their existence on other things and events. My house was built by a carpenter: its coming into existence was dependent on a certain creative activity. Its continued existence is dependent on many things: that a tree does not crush it, that it is not consumed by fire, and so on. If we reflect on the common meaning of the word "God" (no matter how vague and confused this is), we realize that it is incompatible with this meaning that God's existence should *depend* on anything. Whether we believe in Him or not we must admit that the "almighty and everlasting God" (as several ancient prayers begin), the "Maker of heaven and earth, and of all things visible and invisible" (as is said in the Nicene Creed), cannot be thought of as being brought into existence by anything or as depending for His continued existence on anything. To conceive of anything as dependent upon something else for its existence is to conceive of it as a lesser being than God.

If a housewife has a set of extremely fragile dishes, then as dishes they are *inferior* to those of another set like them in all respects except that they are *not* fragile. Those of the first set are *dependent* for their continued existence on gentle handling; those of the second set are not. There is a definite connection in common language between the notions of dependency and inferiority, and independence and superiority. To say that something which was dependent on nothing whatever was superior to ("greater than") anything that was dependent in any way upon anything is quite in keeping with the everyday use of the terms "superior" and "greater." Correlative with the notions of dependence and independence are the notions of *limited* and *unlimited*. An engine requires fuel and this is a limitation. It is the same thing to say that an engine's operation is *dependent* on as that it is *limited* by its fuel supply. An engine that could accomplish the same work in the same time and was in other respects satisfactory, but did not require fuel, would be a *superior* engine.

God is usually conceived of as an *unlimited* being. He is conceived of as a being who *could not* be limited, that is, as an absolutely unlimited being. This is no less than to conceive of Him as *something a greater than which cannot be conceived*. If God is conceived to be an absolutely unlimited being He must be conceived to be unlimited in regard to His existence as well as His operation. In this conception it will not make sense to say that He depends on anything for coming into or continuing in existence. Nor, as Spinoza observed, will it make sense to say that something could *prevent* Him from existing.[12] Lack of moisture can prevent trees from existing in a certain region of the earth. But it would be contrary to the concept of God as an unlimited being to suppose that anything other than God Himself could prevent Him from existing, and it would be self-contradictory to suppose that He Himself could do it.

Some may be inclined to object that although nothing could prevent God's existence, still it might just *happen* that He did not exist. And if He did exist that too would be by chance. I think, however, that from the supposition that it could happen that God did not exist it would follow that, if He existed, He would have mere duration and not eternity. It would make sense to ask, "How long has He existed?," "Will He still exist next week?," "He was in existence yesterday but how about today?," and so on. It seems absurd to make God the subject of such questions. According to our ordinary conception of Him, He is an eternal being. And eternity does not mean endless duration, as Spinoza noted. To ascribe eternity to something is to exclude as senseless all sentences that imply that it has duration. If a thing has duration then it would be merely a *contingent* fact, if it was a fact, that its duration was endless. The moon could have endless duration but not eternity. If something has endless duration it will *make sense* (although it will be false) to say that it will cease to exist, and it will make sense (although it will be false) to say that something will *cause* it to cease to exist. A being with endless duration is not, therefore, an absolutely unlimited being. That God is conceived to be eternal follows from

[12] *Ethics*, pt. I, prop. 11.

the fact that He is conceived to be an absolutely unlimited being.

I have been trying to expand the argument of *Proslogion* 3. In *Responsio* 1 Anselm adds the following acute point: if you can conceive of a certain thing and this thing does not exist then if it *were* to exist its nonexistence would be *possible*. It follows, I believe, that if the thing were to exist it would depend on other things both for coming into and continuing in existence, and also that it would have duration and not eternity. Therefore it would not be, either in reality or in conception, an unlimited being, *aliquid quo nihil maius cogitari possit.*

Anselm states his argument as follows:

> If it [the thing a greater than which cannot be conceived] can be conceived at all it must exist. For no one who denies or doubts the existence of a being a greater than which is inconceivable, denies or doubts that if it did exist its non-existence, either in reality or in the understanding, would be impossible. For otherwise it would not be a being a greater than which cannot be conceived. But as to whatever can be conceived but does not exist: if it were to exist its non-existence either in reality or in the understanding would be possible. Therefore, if a being a greater than which cannot be conceived, can even be conceived, it must exist.[13]

What Anselm has proved is that the notion of contingent existence or of contingent nonexistence cannot have any application to God. His existence must either be logically necessary or logically impossible. The only intelligible way of rejecting Anselm's claim that God's existence is necessary is to maintain that the concept of God, as a being a greater than which cannot be conceived, is self-contradictory or nonsensical.[14] Supposing that this is false, Anselm

[13] *Responsio* 1; Deane, pp. 154–155.

[14] Gaunilo attacked Anselm's argument on this very point. He would not concede that a being a greater than which cannot be conceived existed in his understanding (*Gaunilonis Pro Insipiente*, secs. 4 and 5; Deane, pp. 148–150). Anselm's reply is:

is right to deduce God's necessary existence from his characterization of Him as a being a greater than which cannot be conceived.

Let me summarize the proof. If God, a being a greater than which cannot be conceived, does not exist then He cannot *come* into existence. For if He did He would either have been *caused* to come into existence or have *happened* to come into existence, and in either case He would be a limited being, which by our conception of Him He is not. Since He cannot come into existence, if He does not exist His existence is impossible. If He does exist He cannot have come into existence (for the reasons given), nor can He cease to exist, for nothing could cause Him to cease to exist nor could it just happen that He ceased to exist. So if God exists His existence is necessary. Thus God's existence is either impossible or necessary. It can be the former only if the concept of such a being is self-contradictory or in some way logically absurd. Assuming that this is not so, it follows that He necessarily exists.

It may be helpful to express ourselves in the following way: to say, not that *omnipotence* is a property of God, but rather that *necessary omnipotence* is; and to say, not that omniscience is a property of God, but rather that *necessary omniscience* is. We have criteria for determining that a man knows this and that and can do this and that, and for determining that one man has greater knowledge and abilities in a certain subject than another. We could think of various tests to give them. But there is nothing we should wish to describe, seriously and literally, as "testing" God's knowledge and powers. That God is omniscient and omnipotent has not been determined by the application of criteria: rather these are requirements of our con-

---

"I call on your faith and conscience to attest that this is most false" (*Responsio* 1; Deane, p. 154). Gaunilo's faith and conscience will attest that it is false that "God is not a being a greater than which is inconceivable," and false that "He is not understood (*intelligitur*) or conceived (*cogitatur*)" (*ibid.*). Descartes also remarks that one would go to "strange extremes" who denied that we understand the words *that thing which is the most perfect that we can conceive;* for that is what all men call God" (Haldane and Ross, II, 129).

ception of Him. They are internal properties of the concept, although they are also rightly said to be properties of God. *Necessary existence* is a property of God in the *same sense* that *necessary omnipotence* and *necessary omniscience* are His properties. And we are not to think that "God necessarily exists" means that it follows necessarily from something that God exists *contingently*. The a priori proposition "God necessarily exists" entails the proposition "God exists," if and only if the latter also is understood as an a priori proposition: in which case the two propositions are equivalent. In this sense Anselm's proof is a proof of God's existence.

Descartes was somewhat hazy on the question of whether existence is a property of things that exist, but at the same time he saw clearly enough that *necessary existence* is a property of God. Both points are illustrated in his reply to Gassendi's remark, which I quoted above:

> I do not see to what class of reality you wish to assign existence, nor do I see why it may not be said to be a property as well as omnipotence, taking the word property as equivalent to any attribute or anything which can be predicated of a thing, as in the present case it should be by all means regarded. Nay, necessary existence in the case of God is also a true property in the strictest sense of the word, because it belongs to Him and forms part of His essence alone.[15]

Elsewhere he speaks of "the necessity of existence" as being "that crown of perfections without which we cannot comprehend God."[16] He is emphatic on the point that necessary existence applies solely to "an absolutely perfect Being."[17]

III

I wish to consider now a part of Kant's criticism of the ontological argument which I believe to be wrong. He says:

[15] Haldane and Ross, II, 228.
[16] *Ibid.*, I, 445.
[17] E.g., *ibid.*, Principle 15, p. 225.

If, in an identical proposition, I reject the predicate while retaining the subject, contradiction results; and I therefore say that the former belongs necessarily to the latter. But if we reject subject and predicate alike, there is no contradiction; for nothing is then left that can be contradicted. To posit a triangle, and yet to reject its three angles, is self-contradictory; but there is no contradiction in rejecting the triangle together with its three angles. The same holds true of the concept of an absolutely necessary being. If its existence is rejected, we reject the thing itself with all its predicates; and no question of contradiction can then arise. There is nothing outside it that would then be contradicted, since the necessity of the thing is not supposed to be derived from anything external; nor is there anything internal that would be contradicted, since in rejecting the thing itself we have at the same time rejected all its internal properties. "God is omnipotent" is a necessary judgment. The omnipotence cannot be rejected if we posit a Deity, that is, an infinite being; for the two concepts are identical. But if we say, "There is no God," neither the omnipotence nor any other of its predicates is given; they are one and all rejected together with the subject, and there is therefore not the least contradiction in such a judgment.[18]

To these remarks the reply is that when the concept of God is correctly understood one sees that one cannot "reject the subject." "There is no God" is seen to be a necessarily false statement. Anselm's demonstration proves that the proposition "God exists" has the same a priori footing as the proposition "God is omnipotent."

Many present-day philosophers, in agreement with Kant, declare that existence is not a property and think that this overthrows the ontological argument. Although it is an error to regard existence as a property of things that have contingent existence, it does not follow that it is an error to regard necessary existence as a property of God.

[18] *Op. cit.*, p. 502.

A recent writer says, against Anselm, that a proof of God's existence "based on the necessities of thought" is "universally regarded as fallacious: it is not thought possible to build bridges between mere abstractions and concrete existence."[19] But this way of putting the matter obscures the distinction we need to make. Does "concrete existence" mean contingent existence? Then to build bridges between concrete existence and mere abstractions would be like inferring the existence of an island from the concept of a perfect island, which both Anselm and Descartes regarded as absurd. What Anselm did was to give a demonstration that the proposition "God necessarily exists" is entailed by the proposition "God is a being a greater than which cannot be conceived" (which is equivalent to "God is an absolutely unlimited being"). Kant declares that when "I think a being as the supreme reality, without any defect, the question still remains whether it exists or not."[20] But once one has grasped Anselm's proof of the necessary existence of a being a greater than which cannot be conceived, no question remains as to whether it exists or not, just as Euclid's demonstration of the existence of an infinity of prime numbers leaves no question on that issue.

Kant says that "every reasonable person" must admit that "all existential propositions are synthetic."[21] Part of the perplexity one has about the ontological argument is in deciding whether or not the proposition "God necessarily exists" is or is not an "existential proposition." But let us look around. Is the Euclidean theorem in number theory, "There exists an infinite number of prime numbers," an "existential proposition"? Do we not want to say that *in some sense* it asserts the existence of something? Cannot we say, with equal justification, that the proposition "God necessarily exists" asserts the existence of something, *in some sense?* What we need to understand, in each

[19] J. N. Findlay, "Can God's Existence Be Disproved?," *New Essays in Philosophical Theology*, ed. by A. N. Flew and A. MacIntyre (London, 1955), p. 47 [p. 111 this volume].

[20] *Op. cit.*, pp. 505–506.

[21] *Ibid.*, p. 504.

case, is the particular sense of the assertion. Neither proposition has the same sort of sense as do the propositions, "A low pressure area exists over the Great Lakes," "There still exists some possibility that he will survive," "The pain continues to exist in his abdomen." One good way of seeing the difference in sense of these various propositions is to see the variously different ways in which they are proved or supported. It is wrong to think that all assertions of existence have the same kind of meaning. There are as many kinds of existential propositions as there are kinds of subjects of discourse.

Closely related to Kant's view that all existential propositions are "synthetic" is the contemporary dogma that all existential propositions are contingent. Professor Gilbert Ryle tells us that "Any assertion of the existence of something, like any assertion of the occurrence of something, can be denied without logical absurdity."[22] "All existential statements are contingent," says Mr. I. M. Crombie.[23] Professor J. J. C. Smart remarks that "Existence is not a property" and then goes on to assert that "There can never be any *logical contradiction* in denying that God exists."[24] He declares that "The concept of a logically necessary being is a self-contradictory concept, like the concept of a round square. . . . No existential proposition can be logically necessary," he maintains, for "the truth of a logically necessary proposition depends only on our symbolism, or to put the same thing in another way, on the relationship of concepts" (p. 38). Professor K. E. M. Baier says, "It is no longer seriously in dispute that the notion of a logically necessary being is self-contradictory. Whatever can be conceived of as existing can equally be conceived of as not existing."[25] This is a repetition of Hume's assertion, "Whatever we conceive as existent, we

[22] *The Nature of Metaphysics,* ed. by D. F. Pears (New York, 1957), p. 150.

[23] *New Essays in Philosophical Theology,* p. 114.

[24] *Ibid.,* p. 34.

[25] *The Meaning of Life,* Inaugural Lecture, Canberra University College (Canberra, 1957), p. 8.

can also conceive as non-existent. There is no being, therefore, whose non-existence implies a contradiction."[26]

Professor J. N. Findlay ingeniously constructs an ontological *dis*proof of God's existence, based on a "modern"
view of the nature of "necessity in propositions": the view,
namely, that necessity in propositions "merely reflects our
use of words, the arbitrary conventions of our language."[27]
Findlay undertakes to characterize what he calls "religious
attitude," and here there is a striking agreement between
his observations and some of the things I have said in ex-
pounding Anselm's proof. Religious attitude, he says, pre-
sumes *superiority* in its object and superiority so great that
the worshiper is in comparison as nothing. Religious attitude finds it "anomalous to worship anything *limited* in
any thinkable manner. . . . And hence we are led on irresistibly to demand that our religious object should have
an *unsurpassable* supremacy along all avenues, that it
should tower *infinitely* above all other objects" (p. 51)
[pp. 115–16 this volume]. We cannot help feeling that
"the worthy object of our worship can never be a thing
that merely *happens* to exist, nor one on which all other
objects merely *happen* to depend. The true object of religious reverence must not be one, merely, to which no
actual independent realities stand opposed: it must be one
to which such opposition is totally *inconceivable*. . . .
And not only must the existence of *other* things be unthinkable without Him, but His own non-existence must
be wholly unthinkable in any circumstances" (p. 52) [p.
117 this volume]. And now, says Findlay, when we
add up these various requirements, what they entail is
"not only that there isn't a God, but that the Divine Existence is either senseless or impossible" (p. 54) [pp. 118–
19 this volume]. For on the one hand, "if God is to satisfy
religious claims and needs, He must be a being in every
way inescapable, One whose existence and whose possession of certain excellences we cannot possibly conceive
away." On the other hand, "modern views make it self-

[26] *Dialogues Concerning Natural Religion*, pt. IX.
[27] Findlay, *op. cit.*, p. 54 [p. 119 this volume].

evidently absurd (if they don't make it ungrammatical) to speak of such a Being and attribute existence to Him. It was indeed an ill day for Anselm when he hit upon his famous proof. For on that day he not only laid bare something that is of the essence of an adequate religious object, but also something that entails its necessary nonexistence" (p. 55) [p. 120 this volume].

Now I am inclined to hold the "modern" view that logically necessary truth "merely reflects our use of words" (although I do not believe that the conventions of language are always *arbitrary*). But I confess that I am unable to see how that view is supposed to lead to the conclusion that "the Divine existence is either senseless or impossible." Findlay does not explain how this result comes about. Surely he cannot mean that this view entails that nothing can have necessary properties: for this would imply that mathematics is "senseless or impossible," which no one wants to hold. Trying to fill in the argument that is missing from his article, the most plausible conjecture I can make is the following: Findlay thinks that the view that logical necessity "reflects the use of words" implies, not that nothing has necessary properties, but that *existence* cannot be a necessary property of anything. That is to say, every proposition of the form "*x* exists," including the proposition "God exists," must be *contingent*.[28] At the same time, our concept of God requires that His existence be *necessary*, that is, that "God exists" be a necessary truth. Therefore, the modern view of necessity proves that what the concept of God requires *cannot* be fulfilled. It proves that God *cannot* exist.

The correct reply is that the view that logical necessity merely reflects the use of words cannot possibly have the implication that every existential proposition must be contingent. That view requires us to *look at* the use of words

---

[28] The other philosophers I have just cited may be led to this opinion by the same thinking. Smart, for example, says that "the truth of a logically necessary proposition depends only on our symbolism, or to put the same thing in another way, on the relationship of concepts" (*supra*). This is very similar to saying that it "reflects our use of words."

and not manufacture a priori theses about it. In the Nine-tieth Psalm it is said: "Before the mountains were brought forth, or ever thou hadst formed the earth and the world, even from everlasting to everlasting, thou art God." Here is expressed the idea of the necessary exist-ence and eternity of God, an idea that is essential to the Jewish and Christian religions. In those complex systems of thought, those "languages-games," God has the status of a necessary being. Who can doubt that? Here we must say with Wittgenstein, "This language-game is played!"[29] I believe we may rightly take the existence of those reli-gious systems of thought in which God figures as a neces-sary being to be a disproof of the dogma, affirmed by Hume and others, that no existential proposition can be necessary.

Another way of criticizing the ontological argument is the following. "Granted that the concept of necessary ex-istence follows from the concept of a being a greater than which cannot be conceived, this amounts to no more than granting the *a priori* truth of the *conditional* proposition, 'If such a being exists then it necessarily exists.' This prop-osition, however, does not entail the *existence* of *any-thing*, and one can deny its antecedent without contradic-tion." Kant, for example, compares the proposition (or "judgment," as he calls it) "A triangle has three angles" with the proposition "God is a necessary being." He allows that the former is "absolutely necessary" and goes on to say:

> The absolute necessity of the judgment is only a con-ditional necessity of the thing, or of the predicate in the judgment. The above proposition does not declare that three angles are absolutely necessary, but that, under the condition that there is a triangle (that is, that a triangle is given), three angles will necessarily be found in it.[30]

He is saying, quite correctly, that the proposition about triangles is equivalent to the conditional proposition, "If a

[29] *Philosophical Investigations* (New York, 1953), sec. 654.
[30] *Op. cit.*, pp. 501–502.

triangle exists, it has three angles." He then makes the comment that there is no contradiction "in rejecting the triangle together with its three angles." He proceeds to draw the alleged parallel: "The same holds true of the concept of an absolutely necessary being. If its existence is rejected, we reject the thing itself with all its predicates; and no question of contradiction can then arise."[31] The priest, Caterus, made the same objection to Descartes when he said:

> Though it be conceded that an entity of the highest perfection implies its existence by its very name, yet it does not follow that that very existence is anything actual in the real world, but merely that the concept of existence is inseparably united with the concept of highest being. Hence you cannot infer that the existence of God is anything actual, unless you assume that that highest being actually exists; for then it will actually contain all its perfections, together with this perfection of real existence.[32]

I think that Caterus, Kant, and numerous other philosophers have been mistaken in supposing that the proposition "God is a necessary being" (or "God necessarily exists") is equivalent to the conditional proposition "If God exists then He necessarily exists."[33] For how do they want the

---

[31] *Ibid.*, p. 502.

[32] Haldane and Ross, II, 7.

[33] I have heard it said by more than one person in discussion that Kant's view was that it is really a misuse of language to speak of a "necessary being," on the grounds that necessity is properly predicated only of propositions (judgments) not of *things*. This is not a correct account of Kant. (See his discussion of "The Postulates of Empirical Thought in General," *op. cit.*, pp. 239–256, esp. p. 239 and pp. 247–248.) But if he had held this, as perhaps the above philosophers think he should have, then presumably his view would not have been that the pseudo-proposition "God is a necessary being" is equivalent to the conditional "If God exists then He necessarily exists." Rather his view would have been that the genuine proposition " 'God exists' is necessarily true" is equivalent to the conditional "If God exists then He exists" (*not* "If God exists then He *necessarily* exists,"

antecedent clause, "*If* God exists," to be understood? Clearly they want it to imply that it is *possible* that God does *not* exist.[34] The whole point of Kant's analysis is to try to show that it is possible to "reject the subject." Let us make this implication explicit in the conditional proposition, so that it reads: "If God exists (and it is possible that He does not) then He necessarily exists." But now it is apparent, I think, that these philosophers have arrived at a self-contradictory position. I do not mean that this conditional proposition, taken alone, is self-contradictory. Their position is self-contradictory in the following way. On the one hand, they agree that the proposition "God necessarily exists" is an a priori truth; Kant implies that it is "absolutely necessary," and Caterus says that God's existence is implied by His very name. On the other hand, they think that it is correct to analyze this proposition in such a way that it will entail the proposition "It is possible that God does not exist." But so far from its being the case that the proposition "God necessarily exists" entails the proposition "It is possible that God does not exist," it is rather the case that they are *incompatible* with one another! Can anything be clearer than that the conjunction "God necessarily exists but it is possible that He does not

---

which would be an illegitimate formulation, on the view imaginatively attributed to Kant).

"If God exists then He exists" is a foolish tautology which says nothing different from the tautology "If a new earth satellite exists then it exists." If "If God exists then He exists" were a correct analysis of " 'God exists' is necessarily true," then "If a new earth satellite exists then it exists" would be a correct analysis of " 'A new earth satellite exists' is necessarily true." If the *analysans* is necessarily true then the *analysandum* must be necessarily true, provided the analysis is correct. If this proposed Kantian analysis of " 'God exists' is necessarily true" were correct, we should be presented with the consequence that not only is it necessarily true that God exists, but also it is necessarily true that a new earth satellite exists: which is absurd.

[34] When summarizing Anselm's proof (in part II, *supra*) I said: "If God exists He necessarily exists." But there I was merely stating an entailment. "If God exists" did not have the implication that it is possible He does not exist. And of course I was not regarding the conditional as *equivalent* to "God necessarily exists."

exist" is self-contradictory? Is it not just as plainly self-contradictory as the conjunction "A square necessarily has four sides but it is possible for a square not to have four sides"? In short, this familiar criticism of the ontological argument is self-contradictory, because it accepts *both* of two incompatible propositions.[35]

One conclusion we may draw from our examination of this criticism is that (contrary to Kant) there is a lack of symmetry, in an important respect, between the propositions "A triangle has three angles" and "God has necessary existence," although both are a priori. The former can be expressed in the conditional assertion "If a triangle exists (and it is possible that none does) it has three angles." The latter cannot be expressed in the corresponding conditional assertion without contradiction.

IV

I turn to the question of whether the idea of a being a greater than which cannot be conceived is self-contradictory. Here Leibniz made a contribution to the discussion of the ontological argument. He remarked that the argument of Anselm and Descartes

> is not a paralogism, but it is an imperfect demonstration, which assumes something that must still be proved in order to render it mathematically evident; that is, it is tacitly assumed that this idea of the all-great or all-perfect being is possible, and implies no contradiction. And it is already something that by this remark it is proved that, assuming that God is possible, he exists, which is the privilege of divinity alone.[36]

[35] This fallacious criticism of Anselm is implied in the following remarks by Gilson: "To show that the affirmation of necessary existence is analytically implied in the idea of God, would be . . . to show that God is necessary if He exists, but would not prove that He does exist" (E. Gilson, *The Spirit of Medieval Philosophy*, New York, 1940, p. 62).

[36] *New Essays Concerning the Human Understanding*, Bk. IV, ch. 10; ed. by A. G. Langley (La Salle, Illinois, 1949), p. 504.

Leibniz undertook to give a proof that God is possible. He defined a *perfection* as a simple, positive quality in the highest degree.[37] He argued that since perfections are *simple* qualities they must be compatible with one another. Therefore the concept of a being possessing all perfections is consistent.

I will not review his argument because I do not find his definition of a perfection intelligible. For one thing, it assumes that certain qualities or attributes are "positive" in their intrinsic nature, and others "negative" or "privative," and I have not been able clearly to understand that. For another thing, it assumes that some qualities are intrinsically simple. I believe that Wittgenstein has shown in the *Investigations* that nothing is *intrinsically* simple, but that whatever has the status of a simple, an indefinable, in one system of concepts, may have the status of a complex thing, a definable thing, in another system of concepts.

I do not know how to demonstrate that the concept of God—that is, of a being a greater than which cannot be conceived—is not self-contradictory. But I do not think that it is legitimate to demand such a demonstration. I also do not know how to demonstrate that either the concept of a material thing or the concept of *seeing* a material thing is not self-contradictory, and philosophers have argued that both of them are. With respect to any particular reasoning that is offered for holding that the concept of seeing a material thing, for example, is self-contradictory, one may try to show the invalidity of the reasoning and thus free the concept from the charge of being self-contradictory *on that ground*. But I do not understand what it would mean to demonstrate *in general*, and not in respect to any particular reasoning, that the concept is not self-contradictory. So it is with the concept of God. I should think there is no more of a presumption that it is self-contradictory than is the concept of seeing a material thing. Both concepts have a place in the thinking and the lives of human beings.

But even if one allows that Anselm's phrase may be free of self-contradiction, one wants to know how it can have

[37] See *Ibid.*, Appendix X, p. 714.

any *meaning* for anyone. Why is it that human beings have even *formed* the concept of an infinite being, a being a greater than which cannot be conceived? This is a legitimate and important question. I am sure there cannot be a deep understanding of that concept without an understanding of the phenomena of human life that give rise to it. To give an account of the latter is beyond my ability. I wish, however, to make one suggestion (which should not be understood as autobiographical).

There is the phenomenon of feeling guilt for something that one has done or thought or felt or for a disposition that one has. One wants to be free of this guilt. But sometimes the guilt is felt to be so great that one is sure that nothing one could do oneself, nor any forgiveness by another human being, would remove it. One feels a guilt that is beyond all measure, a guilt "a greater than which cannot be conceived." Paradoxically, it would seem, one nevertheless has an intense desire to have this incomparable guilt removed. One requires a forgiveness that is beyond all measure, a forgiveness "a greater than which cannot be conceived." Out of such a storm in the soul, I am suggesting, there arises the conception of a forgiving mercy that is limitless, beyond all measure. This is one important feature of the Jewish and Christian conception of God.

I wish to relate this thought to a remark made by Kierkegaard, who was speaking about belief in Christianity but whose remark may have a wider application. He says:

> There is only one proof of the truth of Christianity and that, quite rightly, is from the emotions, when the dread of sin and a heavy conscience torture a man into crossing the narrow line between despair bordering upon madness—and Christendom.[38]

One may think it absurd for a human being to feel a guilt of such magnitude, and even more absurd that, if he feels it, he should *desire* its removal. I have nothing to say about that. It may also be absurd for people to fall in love,

[38] *The Journals*, tr. by A. Dru (Oxford, 1938), sec. 926.

but they do it. I wish only to say that there *is* that human phenomenon of an unbearably heavy conscience and that it is importantly connected with the genesis of the concept of God, that is, with the formation of the "grammar" of the word "God." I am sure that this concept is related to human experience in other ways. If one had the acuteness and depth to perceive these connections one could grasp the *sense* of the concept. When we encounter this concept as a problem in philosophy, we do not consider the human phenomena that lie behind it. It is not surprising that many philosophers believe that the idea of a necessary being is an arbitrary and absurd construction.

What is the relation of Anselm's ontological argument to religious belief? This is a difficult question. I can imagine an atheist going through the argument, becoming convinced of its validity, acutely defending it against objections, yet remaining an atheist. The only effect it could have on the fool of the Psalm would be that he stopped saying in his heart "There is no God," because he would now realize that this is something he cannot meaningfully say or think. It is hardly to be expected that a demonstrative argument should, in addition, produce in him a living faith. Surely there is a level at which one can view the argument as a piece of logic, following the deductive moves but not being touched religiously? I think so. But even at this level the argument may not be without religious value, for it may help to remove some philosophical scruples that stand in the way of faith. At a deeper level, I suspect that the argument can be thoroughly understood only by one who has a view of that human "form of life" that gives rise to the idea of an infinitely great being, who views it from the *inside* not just from the outside and who has, therefore, at least some inclination to *partake* in that religious form of life. This inclination, in Kierkegaard's words, is "from the emotions." This inclination can hardly be an *effect* of Anselm's argument, but is rather presupposed in the fullest understanding of it. It would be unreasonable to require that the recognition of Anselm's demonstration as valid must produce a conversion.

B.   A REPLY BY ALVIN PLANTINGA

[*Alvin Plantinga* (1932–   ) *is an associate professor of philosophy at Calvin College. In this piece—one of the many replies called forth by Malcolm's daring article—he argues that Malcolm's attempted rehabilitation of the ontological argument does not succeed.*]

A VALID ONTOLOGICAL ARGUMENT?*

I wish to discuss Professor Malcolm's absorbingly powerful defense of a version of Anselm's ontological proof for the existence of God. Professor Malcolm believes "that in Anselm's *Proslogion* and *Responsio editoris* there are two different pieces of reasoning which he did not distinguish from one another, and that a good deal of light may be shed on the philosophical problem of 'the ontological argument' if we do distinguish them" (p. 136 of this volume). One of these pieces of reasoning is what is usually referred to as Anselm's ontological argument; Malcolm agrees with a tradition beginning with Gaunilo in rejecting that argument. But it is the other argument with which Malcolm is particularly concerned; this one, he believes, is a perfectly sound argument for the existence of God.

I shall not be concerned with the question whether Malcolm has interpreted Anselm correctly, nor shall I discuss his criticism of Kant's refutation of the ontological argument, though I believe that his criticism is mistaken. Instead I shall stick to Malcolm's exposition of this hitherto unnoticed version of the ontological argument, hoping to show that the argument is invalid and that its conclusion (that God's existence is logically necessary) is false. In essence, the proof is an attempt to deduce God's nec-

* From *The Philosophical Review*, Vol. LXX (1961). Reprinted by permission of the Editorial Board of *The Philosophical Review*.

essary existence from our conception of Him as a being than which none greater can be conceived by showing "that the notion of contingent existence or of contingent non-existence cannot have any application to God" (p. 145). Malcolm's account of the proof falls into two parts: an exposition and expansion of Anselm's argument (pp. 141–45) and a summary of it (p. 146). In order to get the argument in its entirety before us, I shall begin by examining the summary.

> Let me summarize the proof. If God, a being a greater than which cannot be conceived, does not exist then He cannot *come* into existence. For if He did He would either have been *caused* to come into existence or have *happened* to come into existence, and in either case He would be a limited being, which by our conception of Him He is not. Since He cannot come into existence, *if He does not exist His existence is impossible* [my italics]. If He does exist He cannot have come into existence (for the reasons given), nor can He cease to exist, for nothing could cause Him to cease to exist nor could it just happen that he ceased to exist. So *if God exists His existence is necessary* [italics mine]. Thus God's existence is either impossible or necessary. It can be the former only if the concept of such a being is self-contradictory or in some way logically absurd. Assuming that this is not so, it follows that He necessarily exists [p. 146].

The structure of the main argument here seems to be the following:

(1) If God does not exist, His existence is logically impossible.

(2) If God does exist, His existence is logically necessary.

(3) Hence either God's existence is logically impossible or it is logically necessary.

(4) If God's existence is logically impossible, the concept of God is contradictory.

(5) The concept of God is not contradictory.

(6) Therefore God's existence is logically necessary.

(3), I take it, is equivalent to the assertion that "the notion of contingent existence or of contingent nonexistence cannot have any application to God" (p. 145); and in fact (3) follows from (1) and (2). Before examining the argument for (1) and (2), however, I wish to consider the intended meaning of the phrase "logically necessary" as it occurs in the proof. A normal inclination would be to understand the assertion "God's existence is logically necessary" as equivalent to the assertion "The proposition 'God exists' is logically necessary." I think this is Malcolm's intention:

> It may be helpful to express ourselves in the following way: to say, not that *omnipotence* is a property of God, but rather that *necessary omnipotence* is; and to say, not that omniscience is a property of God, but rather that *necessary omniscience* is. We have criteria for determining that a man knows this and that and can do this and that, and for determining that one man has greater knowledge and abilities in a certain subject than another. . . . That God is omniscient and omnipotent has not been determined by the application of criteria: rather these are requirements of our conception of Him. They are internal properties of the concept, although they are also rightly said to be properties of God. *Necessary existence* is a property of God in the *same sense* that *necessary omnipotence* and *necessary omniscience* are His properties [pp. 146–47].

It is a requirement of our conception of God that He is omnipotent; it is merely putting this point a different way, I believe, to say that the proposition "God is omnipotent" is logically necessary. The sense in which necessary omnipotence is a property of God is that the proposition "God is omnipotent" is necessary. And necessary existence, says Malcolm, is a property of God in the same sense in which necessary omnipotence and necessary omniscience are. To say "God necessarily exists," then, is to say the same as " 'God exists' is a necessary proposition." This interpretation receives confirmation from the following sentence: "The a priori proposition 'God necessarily exists' entails the proposition 'God exists,' if and only if the latter also is understood as an a priori proposition: in which case the two propositions are equivalent" (p. 147). Taking "logically necessary" and "a priori" as synonyms here, this passage seems to mean that "God necessarily exists" is equivalent to "'God exists' is necessary." I am assuming further that for Malcolm a proposition is logically necessary if and only if its contradictory is self-contradictory. If Malcolm's reconstruction of Anselm's argument is correct, therefore, the proposition "God does not exist" is self-contradictory.

I turn now to premises (1) and (2) of the argument as outlined above. The first step in the argument given in the summary for (1) is to show that from the conception of God as the greatest conceivable being it follows that it is logically impossible for God to come (or to have come) into existence. For if He had either been caused to come into existence, or merely happened to come into existence, He would be a limited being. This inference seems quite correct; it follows from our conception of God that:

(a) N^1 (God never has and never will come into existence).

In the summary Malcolm apparently deduces (1) from (a). But this seems to be a mistake; for (a) does not entail (1) although it entails a proposition similar in some respects to the latter. Taking (a) and the antecedent of (1) as premises and the consequent of (1) as the conclusion, the deduction of (1) from (a) is equivalent to the following argument:

(a) N (God never has and never will come into existence).
(1a) God does not exist—antecedent of (1).
Therefore
(1c) N (God does not exist)—consequent of (1).

[1] The letter "N" before a proposition signifies that the proposition is logically necessary.

But (1c) does not follow from (a) and (1a). What does follow is (1c'): God never will exist. That is, the proposition "It is logically necessary that God never comes into existence" entails:

(1') N (If there is a time at which God does not exist, then there is no subsequent time at which He does exist).

But (1'), of course, cannot play the role assigned to (1) in Malcolm's argument, for (1') cannot help to show that the notion of contingent existence does not apply to God. The argument for (1) in the summary seems invalid, then.

In the exposition of the proof there seem to be two different though related arguments whose conclusions entail (1). I believe that Malcolm's reply to the above criticism would be to appeal to one of these arguments. The one I am referring to runs along the following lines: if God did not exist, and if the fact that He did not were merely contingent, then either He is prevented from existing or He merely happens not to exist. But it is contrary to the concept of God to suppose that anything could prevent Him from existing; and if the supposition that He merely happens not to exist is consistent, then if He did exist He would have "mere duration rather than eternity." But it is a requirement of our concept of God that He is an eternal Being; hence it cannot be true both that God does not exist and that the proposition "God does not exist" is logically contingent. I shall consider this argument after examining the argument in the summary for premise (2) of the proof.

(2) is deduced from (a) (see above) together with (b):

(b) N (God never has and never will cease to exist).

(b), like (a), is deduced from the proposition that God is a being than which no greater can be conceived. Taking (a) and (b) together with the antecedent of (2) as premises and the consequent of (2) as conclusion we get the following inference:

(a) N (God never has and never will begin to exist).
(b) N (God never has and never will cease to exist).
(2a) God exists—antecedent of (2).

Therefore

(2c) N (God exists)—consequent of (2).

Once again it is apparent that (2c) does not follow from (a), (b), and (2a). What does follow is:

(2c′) God always has existed and always will exist.

To put it differently, (a) and (b) together entail the following necessary conditional:

(2′) N (If at *any* time God exists, then at *every* time God exists).

If God cannot (logically) come into or go out of existence, it is a necessary truth that if He ever exists, He always exists. But it does not follow that if He exists, the proposition "God exists" is necessary. The correct definition of "God" might contain or entail that He never comes into or goes out of existence, in which case it would be a necessary truth that He never has and never will either begin or cease to exist. But nothing has been said to show that the fact, if it is a fact, that there is a being so defined is a necessary fact. The argument given in the summary for (2), then, is also invalid.

Allow me to venture a guess as to the origin of the confusion here. One way of advertising the necessary truth of a conditional, in English, is to inject some modal term into the consequent. We might say, for example, "If Jones is a bachelor, he can't be married"; and in so saying, of course, we do not mean to assert that if Jones is a bachelor, the proposition "Jones is unmarried" is necessary. What we do mean is that "If Jones is a bachelor, he is unmarried" is necessary. Similarly here: it is a necessary truth that if God exists, He always has and always will. A normal though misleading way of putting this is to say: if God exists, He cannot fail to exist eternally. But the assertion which is equivalent to my (2′) above, and which does follow from

(a) and (b), should not be confused with (2) which does not so follow.

Now the argument given in the summary for (1) and (2) contains an omission. Malcolm argues that God cannot merely happen to begin to exist nor merely happen to cease to exist, and also that He cannot have been caused either to begin to exist or to cease to exist. But he does not consider the possibility that it just happens that God always has and always will exist (and so happens neither to begin nor cease existing, nor is caused either to begin or cease existing), nor does he consider the possibility that it just happens that God never has existed and never will exist. Malcolm's reply, as I have intimated, is that if either of these were the case, then if God exists, He has mere duration rather than eternity. After arguing that it is contrary to the concept of God to suppose that He depends upon anything for existence or that He could be prevented from existing, Malcolm considers the possibility that God just happens to exist:

> Some may be inclined to object that although nothing could prevent God's existence, still it might just *happen* that He did not exist. And if He did exist that too would be by chance. I think, however, that from the supposition that it could happen that God did not exist it would follow that, if He existed, He would have mere duration and not eternity. It would make sense to ask, "How long has He existed?," "Will He still exist next week?," "He was in existence yesterday but how about today?," and so on. It seems absurd to make God the subject of such questions. According to our ordinary conception of Him, He is an eternal being. And eternity does not mean endless duration, as Spinoza noted. To ascribe eternity to something is to exclude as senseless all sentences that imply that it has duration [p. 144].

The principle of this argument seems to be the contention that if God merely happened to exist He would have duration rather than eternity. In order to see whether the argument holds up we must ask what it is to "happen to exist" and what it is to have mere duration rather than eternity. Now Malcolm appears to be using the locution "happens to exist" in such a way that the proposition "God just happens to exist" is equivalent to the conjunction of the following four propositions:

God just happens to exist ≡ (a) God exists.
(b) "God exists" is logically contingent.
(c) God is not caused to exist.
(d) "God is not caused to exist" is logically necessary.

I am not sure about the inclusion of (d), but my argument will hold without it. The situation with respect to the terms "duration" and "eternity" is not quite so clear, unfortunately. But at any rate the last sentence of the above quotation makes it apparent that if something has eternity, it does not have duration. We must therefore inquire what it is to have duration. First of all it appears that if God had duration it would make sense to ask "How long has He existed?," "He was in existence yesterday, but how about today?," and so forth. Now Malcolm is quite correct, surely, in holding that such questions cannot sensibly be asked about God. But he seems mistaken in inferring the sensibility of these questions from the proposition that God just happens to exist. Let us agree that our normal conception of God includes or entails that He is not caused to exist and that His existence has neither beginning nor end. It will then be true and necessarily true that:

(7) If God exists, then there is a being whose existence is not caused and who has neither beginning nor end.

The whole conditional is necessary, but we have no reason so far for supposing that either its antecedent or its consequent is. It may be a logically contingent truth, if it is a truth, that there actually is a being so conceived. And if God, so defined, does exist, the four conditions I suggested as constituting the meaning of "God happens to exist" will all be fulfilled. But the question "How long has God existed?" will not "make sense." For in asking the question one implies that He does exist. And the assertion that God exists entails the assertion that He has always existed. Hence anyone who understands the question already knows the answer; to ask that question seriously is to betray misapprehension of the concept of God. Similarly the question "Will He still exist next week?" will be absurd. For it also implies that He does exist; but in the conception suggested above the conjunction "He does exist now, but next week He will no longer exist" is contradictory. Hence I conclude that "God merely happens to exist" does not entail that God has duration in any sense involving the logical propriety of questions of the sort Malcolm mentions.

Further on in the same passage, however, there seems to be a slightly different sense of "duration" introduced:

> If a thing has duration then it would be merely a *contingent* fact, if it was a fact, that its duration was endless. The moon could have endless duration but not eternity. If something has endless duration it will *make sense* (although it will be false) to say that it will cease to exist, and it will make sense (although it will be false) to say that something will *cause* it to cease to exist. A being with endless duration is not, therefore, an absolutely unlimited being [p. 144].

Here it is suggested that the assertion "God has duration" has three components. That assertion entails (a) that any statement specifying the temporal limits of God's existence is contingent, (b) that "God will cease to exist" is sensible, and (c) that "God will be caused to cease to exist" is sensible. (c) appears to entail (b); perhaps it is also meant to entail (a), but I leave that question on one side. Now it seems clear that the proposition "God merely happens to exist," understood as above, does not entail (b). If an adequate definition of "God" includes or entails that He never comes into or goes out of existence, it obviously will not "make sense" to suppose that God will cease to exist. For "God will cease to exist" entails "There is a time at which God exists and a later time at which He does not." But under the definition in question that proposition is contradictory. Hence the supposition that God merely happens to exist does not entail (b). Nor does it entail (c), since (c) entails (b).

The situation with respect to (a) is a bit more complicated. Suppose we take the assertion:

(8) God has neither beginning nor end

as a specification of God's temporal limits in the somewhat Pickwickian sense that it denies any such limits to His existence. There are two possible interpretations of this proposition:

(8a) If God exists, then He has always existed and will always exist; and

(8b) God does exist and He always has existed and always will exist.

On the interpretation I have been suggesting, (8a) is logically necessary; (8b) is contingent, though each of its conjuncts entails the remaining two. Accepting the second interpretation of (8), then, we might say that the proposition "God merely happens to exist" entails that God has duration. But this is a weak sense indeed of "duration"; in fact to say that God has duration in that sense is to say no more than that "God exists" is logically contingent—which, after all, was the essential component of the contention that God merely happens to exist. In particular this in no way implies that questions of the sort Malcolm mentions are legitimate; nor does having duration in this sense constitute a limitation. It is a mistake, therefore, to suppose that God's happening to exist is inconsistent with His being "that than which none greater can be conceived."

Malcolm supports the argument I have just criticized by an exegesis of a passage in Anselm's *Responsio I:*

In *Responsio I* Anselm adds the following acute point: if you can conceive of a certain thing and this thing does not exist then if it *were* to exist its nonexistence would be *possible*. It follows, I believe, that if the thing were to exist it would depend on other things both for coming into and continuing in existence, and also that it would have duration and not eternity. Therefore it would not be, either in reality or in conception, an unlimited being [p. 145].

The first point here seems to be that the proposition "God can be conceived but does not exist" entails the proposition "If God existed, His nonexistence would be possible." This seems correct. But Malcolm draws the further inference that if God were to exist, then He would "depend upon other things" and would have mere duration rather than eternity. This argument comes to the following:

(9) If the existence of God were logically contingent, God would depend upon other beings both for coming into existence and for continuing in existence, and God would have duration rather than eternity.

I believe I have already shown that from the supposition that God's existence is logically contingent it does not follow that He has duration rather than eternity, except in the trivial sense in which predicating duration of God is saying no more than that the proposition "God exists" is logically contingent. But it seems equally clear that God's dependence upon other things does not follow from the supposition that His existence is logically contingent. Malcolm states his argument in such a way that any statement of contingent existence entails that the subject of the statement depends upon other things both for coming into and for continuing in existence. But this is surely a mistake. For all we know, certain elementary physical particles—for example, electrons—may always have existed, in which case they surely don't depend upon anything for coming into existence. And for all we know there may be nothing upon which they depend for their continued existence. But of course it would not follow from the truth of these suppositions that the statement "Electrons don't exist" is self-contradictory, or that the existence of electrons is logically necessary.

Perhaps Malcolm had the following in mind here: even if electrons depend upon nothing at all for coming into or continuing in existence the assertion that they do not so depend is contingent. But the assertion that God does not depend upon anything is necessary. And it is inconsistent to hold both that God's existence is contingent and that it is a necessary truth that He depends upon nothing at all either for coming into or for continuing in existence. I think this is the heart of Malcolm's argument. But I must confess inability to see the inconsistency. Malcolm is entirely correct in taking it that the proposition "God does not depend upon anything for coming into or continuing in existence" is logically necessary. As he says, the necessity of this proposition follows from the fact that God is conceived, in the Hebraic-Christian tradition, as a being than which nothing greater can be conceived. And hence an adequate definition of the word "God" must include or entail that He is dependent upon nothing whatever. But the assertion that a being so defined exists, that the definition actually applies to something, may well be, for all that Malcolm and Anselm have said, a contingent assertion. It is a necessary truth that if God exists, then there is a being who neither comes into nor goes out of existence and who is in no way dependent upon anything else. But from this it does not follow, contrary to Malcolm's argument, that the proposition "There is a being who neither comes into nor goes out of existence and who depends upon nothing" is necessary; nor does it follow that "God exists" is necessary. Malcolm's reconstruction of the ontological argument therefore fails.

C. A REPLY BY PAUL HENLE

[*Paul Henle (1908–1962), a professor of philosophy at the University of Michigan for many years, was well known for his work in logic, philosophy of science, and allied topics. Here Henle, with the wit and force so characteristic of his writing, argues that Malcolm's restatement of the ontological argument is unsound.*]

USES OF THE ONTOLOGICAL ARGUMENT*

That anyone should uphold the ontological argument as demonstrative of the existence of God is surprising, yet Professor Norman Malcolm seems perfectly serious in his recent defense of one form of it. He maintains that the argument has two variants, one, which he rejects, concludes that God exists and the other, which he accepts, maintains that God has necessary existence. This acceptance is the more remarkable because Malcolm does not base his contention on any Neoplatonic identification of existence with reality and fullness of being. Granted such a metaphysics, the argument would seem to follow, but Malcolm does not take this approach and indeed professes to have difficulty in comprehending the doctrine of negation and privation characteristic of it (p. 157 of this volume). Without such metaphysical buttressing, the argument is quite weak, but it may be well first to show that something is wrong with it before going on to consider what is wrong.

I

Gaunilo was on the right track with his query as to why the same reasoning did not prove the existence of the most perfect island conceivable,[1] and it must be noticed that Anselm in his reply does not present any argument but merely asserts that the reasoning may be applied only to God.[2] If Anselm was implying, in accordance with Neo-

* From *The Philosophical Review*, Vol. LXX (1961). Reprinted by permission of Mrs. Jeanne Henle and the Editorial Board of *The Philosophical Review*.
[1] Gaunilo, *Pro Insipiente*, Sect. 6, trans. by S. N. Deane in *St. Anselm* (La Salle, Ill., 1903), pp. 150–151.
[2] "Appendix to Proslogium," ch. III, in Deane, *op. cit.*, p. 159.

platonic principles, that a perfect island is a contradiction in terms, the objection is well taken. Still, a better counter-example than Gaunilo's can be given and we may turn to it.

Let us designate by *"Nec"* a certain being who has necessary existence but who is otherwise less remarkable. He has a certain amount of knowledge, though nothing extraordinary, and certain power, though he is unable to cause motion. As a necessary being, of course, *Nec*'s non-existence is inconceivable and he does not depend on anything. *Nec* is limited in the sense that his knowledge is exceeded by that of other beings, but it is not limited in the sense in which an engine is limited by its fuel supply; in this latter sense, which is very like dependence, he is unlimited. Clearly *Nec* cannot exist contingently since he is a being whose nonexistence is inconceivable. He cannot, therefore, merely happen to exist, nor can he exist temporally for reasons which Malcolm has explained in a parallel argument (pp. 143–44). It follows that *Nec* must exist necessarily or else it is impossible that he exist at all, and assuming what seems plausible, that there is no inherent contradiction in his nature, *Nec* must exist.

For a traditional theist, *Nec* creates some perplexity for, if God is omnipotent, he can create or destroy *Nec*. But if, as was explained, *Nec* is an absolutely necessary being, nothing can create or destroy him. Hence, clearly, if *Nec* exists there is no omnipotent deity and, equally clearly, if there is an omnipotent deity, *Nec* does not exist. Since, however, the proof of the existence of one is parallel to the proof of the existence of the other, it is a little difficult to know what to think.

Even though *Nec*'s existence precludes that of an omnipotent being, it is perfectly compatible with that of other beings having necessary existence. *Nec* has a big brother,[3] *NEc*, who also exists necessarily but who can cause uniform rectilinear motion and is a little wiser than *Nec*. There is another brother, *NEC*, who can cause accelera-

[3] Size and fraternity are ascribed metaphorically.

tion, and only typographic inadequacies prevent my enumerating a spate of others.

Nec and all his family would of course be disposed of summarily by any Neoplatonist. If necessary existence is independent existence, it can be possessed only by what is completely perfect, and this at once is the omniscient and omnipotent. But Malcolm is not arguing on the basis of Neoplatonism and is merely speaking of a necessarily existing, independent and, in this special sense, unlimited being. It may be that these qualities entail having more than mediocre power and knowledge, but we are not given an argument to this effect.

II

Clearly something is wrong. One does not want to admit the existence of *Nec* and his confreres, but where is the fallacy? There seems to be nothing inconsistent in the description of *Nec* and, since he cannot exist contingently, he must exist necessarily. Perhaps the difficulty is to be solved by an analysis of the notion of a necessary being. If we say "Necessary existence is a property of *Nec*," the term "necessary" may be construed in two senses; in one, it would modify the statement as a whole, in the other it would modify "being." The first interpretation would make the sentence equivalent to "It is necessary that existence is a property of *Nec*." Thus what would be attributed to *Nec* would be simply existence in an ordinary sense, but it would be held that he possesses this existence necessarily.

Malcolm cannot have this sense in mind for, if it is applied to statements about God, it reduces his second form of the ontological argument to the first. It merely ascribes existence to God and though it claims that the ascription is necessary, it is no different from the form of the argument which he repudiates. His intention must be to say that "necessary" qualifies "existence."

This adjectival use of "necessary" is of course common, as when one says "Tom would be a good scholar if he had the necessary patience." In this case, however, the term is relative and one can properly ask for what it is necessary. The necessary patience is simply the patience which is required if one is to be a scholar. It is not that there are two sorts of patience, ordinary patience and necessary patience, and however patient Tom may be in the ordinary sense—however steadfast, pertinacious, and unswerving in the pursuit of a goal—he can never become a scholar because he lacks this special virtue of necessary patience.

Other adjectival uses of "necessary" seem to be of the same relative sort. A necessary condition, to take another example, is always a necessary condition of something and it is necessary for the existence of that thing. It is not that there are two sorts of conditions, necessary and ordinary, and that some events have necessary conditions and some ordinary. Again, it is sometimes said that death is a necessary evil and once more it seems fair to ask for what it is necessary. "For the existence of life" or "for the perfection of the world" are two conventional answers, each giving some external goal which is served by death. Even when Kant speaks of space and time as necessary ideas, he seems to mean that human thought requires them, that is, that they are necessary for the exercise of our intuition.

Malcolm not merely attributes necessary existence to God, but also necessary omnipotence and necessary omniscience (p. 146). It is natural to ask for what the omnipotence is necessary. It will not do to say that the omnipotence is necessary for consistent discourse or for the existence of God, because these would simply be indirect ways of saying that the statement "God is omnipotent" is a necessary statement and this interpretation has been rejected. It will not do either to name some external end for which God's omnipotence is necessary as if one were to say, "God has the necessary omnipotence to inspire awe." One is driven to the reluctant conclusion that Malcolm believes that necessary omnipotence is a special variety of omnipotence. One is then compelled to inquire what is the differentia of this sort of omnipotence and, in particular, what can a being which has necessary omnipotence do which a being that merely has omnipotence cannot.

III

I must confess to being completely baffled by Malcolm's use of "necessary." I do not on that account, however, wish to suggest that he is wrong. It may be that at some time an explanation will be forthcoming and it will develop that there is no objection to speaking of necessary beings. Then we will once more be confronted with the existence of *Nec* and his family of necessary beings. We must seek another way of getting rid of them.

Perhaps the difficulty lies in the use of the name *Nec*. Russell, of course, claimed that it is meaningless to use a proper name without assuming the existence of whatever is named. If *Nec* is regarded as a proper name, then on Russell's theory any statement about *Nec* would assume that he exists. Russell would claim that *Nec* is not a proper name for those of us who have not met *Nec*, but is merely an abbreviation of a definite description. According to Russell's view, any statement using the description implies the existence of *Nec* and, according to other theories, it presupposes his existence, so in either case the question at issue seems to have been prejudged. Even without getting into discussions of the theory of proper names and of descriptions, most people use proper names only when they think they are naming something. It is not necessary to argue that this is the only way in which names can be used, but merely that one expects the existence and may be misled by its lack. Perhaps, then, it would be well to focus attention on the use of the proper name.

One way would be to challenge the existential assumption directly by saying something like "If *Nec* exists, he exists necessarily." This might be thought to call *Nec*'s existence into question rather than to assume it. Malcolm, however, would regard this as illegitimate and as involving something like a pragmatic contradiction.[4] The very use of the conditional form implies that it is possible that *Nec* does not exist, but clearly, by his very nature, he does. Some alternative procedure must be tried.

[4] This is how I understand his argument on pp. 154–56.

We noticed that *Nec* is not the only being whose existence can be proved in the manner indicated, and perhaps, instead of concentrating on him, we should enter into a more general discussion. This will not merely dispose of our problem wholesale but will also get rid of the influence of proper names since one must use a generic description in speaking of the whole group. Let us refer to beings having necessary existence as *necessary beings* and see what statements can be made about them all. It is tempting to speak of "all necessary beings" but the locution is better avoided because "all" itself raises questions of existential import which cannot but hinder the discussion. Such a phrase as "whatever necessary beings there are" is of a common enough form to be readily intelligible and still of a form which leaves the matter of existence open. It does not imply that there are necessary beings, but neither does it imply that there are none. Thus we may assert that whatever necessary beings there are have necessary existence. This will be admitted at once as true by definition. Again, whatever necessary beings there are exist independently of anything else. Here, once more, there will be no question. Whatever necessary beings there are are not limited by anything else. Surely. Whatever necessary beings there are cannot exist contingently. No doubt. Whatever necessary beings there are cannot begin to exist. This perhaps involves some additional assumptions, but it may be granted. So with any of the other statements we have discussed, but none of this proves the existence of *Nec* or of any other necessary beings. It merely describes any that may exist.

There was no relevant property ascribed to *Nec* in the first description of him which was not attributed to necessary beings in general, yet there is clearly no temptation to conclude from the description of necessary beings that they exist. If then there was any inclination to believe in the existence of *Nec*, it must have been merely because of the use of the proper name. Since proper names usually or always imply or presuppose existence, it is easy to slide into the belief that what has been named exists, and this is particularly easy when the entity in question is described in terms of existence. But surely nothing is proved by the mere introduction of a proper name.

We have tried using the device of quantification to get rid of any assumption of existence inherent in the use of a proper name, and so far it has led to the conclusion that the argument begs the question. There is, however, another mode of quantification, the existential, which remains to be tried. What of the statement "There is at least one being having necessary existence?" Can it be contingently true? Malcolm thinks not. Is it impossible? Again Malcolm believes not. Must it not then be necessarily true? I confess I do not know. Since, as indicated before, I have no idea what is meant by "necessary existence," the whole question seems completely befogged.

One point, however, does stand out as clear, namely, that even if the statement, "There is at least one being having necessary existence," is itself taken to be necessarily true, it does not follow that *Nec* exists, or *NEc*, or any other necessary being. To establish the existence of any one necessary being something more is needed than the existence of some such. There does not seem to be any reason for the existence of *Nec* which is not merely a reason for saying that some necessary being exists. To use this reason for the specific conclusion about *Nec* would be fallacious and the fallacy would be the same as before: begging the question. The alternative of existential quantification thus leads back to the same conclusion as before. In the one case as in the other only the use of *Nec*'s name makes his existence plausible.

Something of the same sort, I am convinced, has happened in Malcolm's form of the ontological argument. If he restated his claims using "all gods" or "whatever deities there are" in place of the proper name I do not believe he would arrive at the existence of anything. If he argued that there must be a being having necessary existence—whatever necessary existence may be—I do not believe he could conclude the existence of any specific being. The mere introduction of a proper name seems to be the sole basis for drawing his conclusion. This confusion is rendered easier because "God" functions sometimes as a proper name and sometimes as a generic term as in "There is no God." But the confusion is the same that there was with *Nec* and the question is begged.

IV

Begging the question is not, of course, a formal fallacy. There is nothing invalid in concluding what one has already assumed. It does, however, place severe limitations on the use which can be made of an argument. Thus if no one who did not already believe in God would admit the premise that God is a necessary being, there would be little use in advancing it to convince anyone that God exists. There are, however, other uses of argument besides convincing people; they may serve to remind one of his beliefs and to summarize them. This is the function which Anselm sometimes at least assigned to the ontological argument. He insisted that reason is not the basis of faith but presupposes faith and exists for the clarification of faith. "For I do not seek to understand that I may believe, but I believe in order to understand. For this I also believe—that unless I believed I should not understand."[5] From this point of view, the argument serves not to convert but to clarify the convictions of the converted, and begging the question is no obstacle. Again, at the beginning of his reply to Gaunilo, Anselm says:

> It was a fool against whom the argument of my Proslogium was directed. Seeing, however, that the author of these objections is by no means a fool and is a Catholic speaking in behalf of the fool, I think it is sufficient that I answer the Catholic.[6]

Much the same situation obtains in regard to Descartes' use of the ontological argument. In the *Meditations*, which he took to be the definitive exposition of his metaphysical

---

[5] *Proslogium*, ch. I, in Deane, *op. cit.*, p. 7.
[6] "Appendix," Deane, *op. cit.*, p. 153.

position,[7] he uses the ontological argument only after he has affirmed the existence of God by another argument. M. Guéroult has argued with considerable ingenuity that this order is irreversible.[8] As used in *Meditation V* the ontological argument claims that the existence of God is as evident as the truths of mathematics. This would have proved nothing, however, unless the truths of mathematics had been vindicated by a prior proof of the existence of God. Thus the function of the ontological argument can only be to summarize and encapsulate what was proved before.

From all these considerations it would appear not merely that the ontological argument not only cannot produce conviction where none existed before, but also was not intended to by some of its more prominent exponents. This is the reason that, as Malcolm notices at the end of his paper, an atheist might recognize the validity of the argument and still not be converted. He would recognize the validity but not the truth of the premises, and so would find in the argument no more than a simple exercise in hypothetical reasoning. Thus not merely is Malcolm right in concluding that "It would be unreasonable to require that the recognition of Anselm's demonstration as valid must produce a conversion," but one may go further and say that it would be unreasonable to expect that the argument should produce the slightest change in belief.

[7] Cf. Preface to the *Principles of Philosophy* where Descartes suggests that one read his *Meditations* to get a better understanding of the *Principles*.

[8] *Nouvelles réflexions sur la preuve ontologique de Descartes* (Paris, 1955), pp. 22 ff.